AF848557

BREAST MILK COMPONENTS AND NEURODEVELOPMENTAL RISK IN CHILDREN BORN TO MOTHERS WITH PREECLAMPSIA

Acknowledgement

I had decided to enroll for my PhD in the year 2012 and today this journey is complete. During this journey there were people who helped me directly or indirectly in achieving the completion of my PhD work. I would like to take this opportunity to thank one and all who accompanied me in this journey. First and foremost, my utmost gratitude to Dr. Sadhana Joshi Head of our Department who guided me in shaping the research work presented in this thesis. I thank her for the kind and patient guidance, encouragement and precious direction which inspired a great enthusiasm in me for the completion of this project. We have worked together in areas other than this thesis work which has been an intense learning experience.

My deepest gratitude to my guide Dr. Preeti Chavan-Gautam for her timely guidance and interest in my research which has greatly motivated me. Words can't explain my thankfulness for Dr. Anitha Killari and Dr. Anvita Kale. They have supported and guided me through the crucial years of my PhD. They helped me a lot in practical issues in the laboratory. I thank them for their unconditional support, timely motivation, sympathetic attitude and unfailing help during the course of this entire study.

I also thank Prof. Emeritus Dr. S. P. Mahadik, Department of Psychiatry and Health Behavior, Georgia Regents University, Augusta, USA for his suggestions throughout this research work.

No research is possible without infrastructure and requisite materials and resource. My sincere thanks to Dr. Akhilesh Chandra Mishra, Director, IRSHA, Bharati Vidyapeeth (Deemed to be University), Pune and former Director, Prof. Prabhakar Ranjekar, who gave me an opportunity to work at Mother and Child Health Department.

I would like to extend my gratitude to the clinicians, Prof. Dr. Savita Mehendale (Department of Obstetrics and Gynaecology) and Prof. Dr.Sanjay Lalwani (Department of Paediatrics) Bharati Hospital, Pune. I am also very grateful to the participants of the study.

I am immensely indebted to my colleagues at the Mother and child Health Department, Hemlata who helped me achieve my goal, Vidya for keeping a friendly environment during the lab work, Vrushali and Shruti K for their moral support and motivation throughout the course and Karuna for her help in the strenuous statistical analysis for this study. I would like to thank my colleagues Deepali, Nisha, Harsha, Pratiksha, Vandita, Amrita, Richa, Nisha K, Vinita, Akriti, Alka, Shruti J, Surbhi S, Anjali, Vaishali, Anindita, Kinjal, Juhi, Mayur, Rahat, Anupam, Sakshi, Shweta, Surabhi, Prachi I, Prachi J, Shridevi, Vandana and Sagar who shared their experiences and helped me throughout the study. My special thanks to Dr. Amrita for helping me in compiling my thesis.

A special acknowledgement to the administrative and non- scientific staff Mrs. Kadam, Mr. Gavade, Mr. Patil, Mrs. Gajare, Mr. Nitin, Tushar, Deshmukh, Ajay and Ravindra.

I would like to acknowledge the financial support given by Indian Council of Medical Research (ICMR) for carrying out my research work. I would also like to extend my sincere gratitude to Dr. Naranamangalam R. Jagannathan, All India Institute of Medical Sciences, AIIMS, New Delhi, for providing us the facility to carry out the NMR studies.

Words cannot express how grateful I am to my parents, parent-in-laws, sisters and brothers for their sacrifices, constant encouragement, and heartfelt support throughout my journey. I fall short of words while expressing my feelings towards my husband Dhanesh, who inspired me in my journey and has supporting me in every facet of life. My beloved son Arnav for his patience which he showed during my thesis writing. I thank god for giving me such a lovely and caring family, who stood beside me with their love and unconditional support.

I also thank "The Almighty" who has given me patience, health, wisdom and blessings to accomplish this thesis.

Thank you, Lord !!!

……Kamini

THESIS AT A GLANCE

Breast Milk Components and Neurodevelopmental Risk in Children Born to Mothers with Preeclampsia

Chapters

- Introduction
- Aim and Objectives
- Review of Literature
- Materials and Methods
- Results
- Discussion
- Conclusion

Publications

- Clinica Chimica Acta
2016; 12:75-83
Impact factor 2.87
- International Journal of Developmental Neuroscience
2014; 33:115-121
Impact factor 2.04
- International Journal of Developmental Neuroscience
2013; 31:209-213
Impact factor 2.04

Conferences

- 20th Annual SNEHA-MRC International Workshop, Pune.
February, 2017
- 7th International Conference on Growing Trends in Food Technology and Nutrition for Public Health Care, New Delhi
May, 2016
- 45th Annual National Conference of Nutrition Society of India. (NSI)
November, 2013

Award

First Prize

Oral Presentation

7th International Conference on Growing Trends in Food Technology and Nutrition for Public Health Care
New Delhi

May, 2016

Index

Chapter 1 Introduction

1.1 Breast Milk and Infant Growth 1

1.2 Factors Affecting Breast Milk Composition 2

1.2.1 Stage of Lactation 3

1.2.2 Pregnancy Complications 3

1.3 Effect of Breastfeeding on Brain Development of Infant 4

1.4 Components of Breast Milk and Brain Development in Children 5

1.4.1 Milk Fatty Acids and Brain Development in Children 5

1.4.2 Milk Amino Acids and Brain Development in Children 6

1.4.3 Milk Choline and Brain Development in Children 6

1.4.4 Milk Lactose and Brain Development in Children 7

1.4.5 Milk Neurotrophins and Brain Development in Children 7

1.5 Genesis of the Thesis 8

1.6 Hypothesis 10

Chapter 2 Aim and Objectives

2.1 Aim 11

2.2 Objectives 11

Chapter 3 Review of Literature

3.1 Importance of Breast Milk 12

3.2 Global Strategy for Breastfeeding 12

3.2.1 Breastfeeding and Associated Outcomes 13

3.3 Anatomy of the Breast 15

3.4 Lactogenesis 16

3.5 Breast Milk Composition 17

3.5.1 Fats 17

3.5.2 Carbohydrates 22

3.5.3 Protein 23
3.5.4 Choline 24
3.5.5 Vitamins and Minerals 25
3.5.6 Other Bioactive Factors 25
3.5.7 Neurotrophins 26
3.6 Factors Influencing Human Milk 28
3.7 Preeclampsia 34
3.7.1 Pathophysiology of Preeclampsia 34
3.8 The Developmental Origins of Health and Adult Disease (DOHaD) 38
3.8.1 Consequences of Preeclampsia on Mother and their Children 39
3.8.2 Preeclampsia and Risk for Neurodevelopment Disorders of Children 41
3.9 Brain Development 41
3.9.1 Embryonic and Fetal Brain Development 42
3.9.2 Postnatal Brain Development 43
3.9.3 Nutrition and Brain Functioning 43
3.10 Breastfeeding and Neurodevelopment in Children 44
3.10.1 Breast Milk Fatty Acids and Brain Development in Children 46
3.10.2 Breast Milk Neurotrophins and Brain Development in Children 46
3.10.3 Milk Metabolites and Brain Development in Children 47
3.11 Cognition 47
3.12 Cognitive tests 48
Chapter 4 Materials and Methods
4.1 Ethics Approval and Enrolment 53
4.1.1 Inclusion Criteria 53
4.1.2 Exclusion Criteria 53
4.1.3 Definition and Diagnosis of Preeclampsia 53
4.2 Dietary Assessments 54

4.3 Collection and Storage of Samples 54

4.3.1 Follow up of Infant 55

4.4 Biochemical Estimations 56

4.4.1 Plasma and Milk Fatty acids 56

4.4.2 Plasma and Milk Nerve Growth Factor (NGF) 56

4.4.3 Plasma and Milk Brain Derived Neurotrophic Factor (BDNF) 57

4.4.4 Milk Metabolites 57

4.5 Anthropometric Measurement of Infant 59

4.6 Cognitive Assessment of Children 60

4.7 Power of the Study 61

4.8 Inter and Intra Assay Variability 61

4.9 Statistical Analysis 61

Chapter 5 Results

5.1 Maternal and Neonatal Characteristics 62

5.2 Frequency of Consumption of ALA, DHA and Omega-3 Fatty Acid Rich Foods 63

5.3 Maternal Plasma LCPUFA Levels 63

5.4 Maternal Plasma Neurotrophin Levels (BDNF and NGF) 63

5.5 Milk Fatty Acid Levels in Control and Preeclampsia Groups at Various Time Points of Lactation 64

5.6 Milk Fatty Acid Levels in Women Consuming Vegetarian and Non-Vegetarian Diets 66

5.7 Milk Neurotrophin Levels in Control and Preeclampsia Groups at Various Time Points of Lactation 67

5.8 Milk Neurotrophins Levels in Women Consuming Vegetarian and Non-Vegetarian Diets 68

5.9 Metabolic Profile of Milk 68

5.9.1 Multivariate Analysis 70

5.10 Levels of Milk Metabolites 72

5.11 Levels of Milk Metabolites in Women Consuming Vegetarian and Non-vegetarian Diets 75

5.12 Associations of Milk Fatty Acids with Baby Characteristics during Lactation 75

5.13 Associations of Milk Neurotrophins with Baby Characteristics during Lactation 76

5.14 Associations of Milk Neurotrophins with Milk Fatty Acids 76

5.15 Anthropometric Measurement in Children from Birth to 3-6 yrs of Age 76

5.15.1 Standard Score of Index of the KABC-II 77

5.16 Associations of Milk Fatty Acids with Cognition of Children 78

Chapter 6 Discussion

6.1 Maternal Plasma and Milk Fatty Acid Levels in Control and Preeclampsia Groups at Various Time Points of Lactation 79

6.2 Maternal Plasma and Milk Neurotrophin Levels in Control and Preeclampsia Groups at Various Time Points of Lactation 81

6.3 Associations of Milk Fatty Acids with Baby Characteristics during Lactation 85

6.4 Levels of Milk Metabolites 85

6.5 Anthropometric Measurements in Children from Birth to 3-6 yrs of Age....88

6.6 Cognitive Performance of Children 89

Summary 91

Conclusion 97

Bibliography 98

Publications 144

Award 145

Conferences 146

List of Tables

Table 1: Tests of Cognition.. 48

Table 2: Subtests of Kaufman Assessment Battery 60

Table 3: Maternal and Neonatal Characteristics.. 62

Table 4: The Concentration of Metabolites in Milk (mM/L) from Controls and Women with Preeclampsia at Day 3 and at 6 Months of Lactation........ 74

Table 5: Anthropometric Measurement in Children at 3-6 yrs of Age................. 76

Table 6: Standard Score of Index of the KABC-II at 3-6 yrs of Age 77

List of Figures

Figure 1: Breast Milk Components and Infant Growth 1
Figure 2: Factors Affecting Breast Milk Composition 2
Figure 3: Components of Breast Milk and Brain Development in Children 5
Figure 4: Global Distribution of Breastfeeding at 12 Months 13
Figure 5: Benefits of Breastfeeding to the Infant 14
Figure 6: Structure of Mammary gland 15
Figure 7: Structure of a Fatty Acid (e.g. Palmitic acid; C16:0) 18
Figure 8: Types of Fatty Acids 19
Figure 9: Biosynthesis of Polyunsaturated Fatty Acids 22
Figure 10: Neurotrophins and Their Receptors 27
Figure 11: Pathogenesis of Preeclampsia 35
Figure 12: Concept of Developmental Origins of Health and Diseases and Risk for Diseases 38
Figure 13: Short Term and Long Term Consequences of Preeclampsia 40
Figure 14: Timeline of Major Events in Brain Development 42
Figure 15: Breast Milk Components and Brain Development of Children 44
Figure 16: Structure of KBAC II 49
Figure 17: Face Recognition 50
Figure 18: Word Order 50
Figure 19: Atlantis 51
Figure 20: Pattern Reasoning 51
Figure 21: Expressive Vocabulary 52
Figure 22: Flow Chart Showing the Number of Milk Samples Analyzed for Fatty Acids, Neurotrophins and Other Metabolites at Various Time points During Lactation 55
Figure 23: Maternal Plasma Neurotrophins Levels 63
Figure 24: Milk Fatty Acids Levels at Various Time Points of Lactation 65
Figure 25: Milk Fatty Acid Levels at Day 3 in Women Consuming Vegetarian and Non-vegetarian Diets 66
Figure 26: Milk Fatty Acid Levels at 6 month in Women Consuming Vegetarian and Non-vegetarian Diets 67

Figure 27: Milk Neurotrophin Levels at Various Time Points of Lactation................68
Figure 28: 1D ^{1}H NMR Spectrum of Milk of Women with Preeclampsia..................69
Figure 29: Multivariate Analysis Plots Showing Clusters of Milk Samples from Control and Preeclampsia Groups at Day 3 and 6 mo of Lactation................71
Figure 30: Multivariate Analysis Plots Showing Clusters of Milk Samples from Preeclampsia and Control Groups 72
Figure 31: Standard Score of Index of the KABC-II in Preeclampsia Groups based on Gestation 77

CHAPTER 1
INTRODUCTION

1.1 Breast Milk and Infant Growth

Maternal nutritional status is a strong determinant of growth and development of the fetus and infant during the first 1000 days of life (Cetin and Laoreti, 2015; Wrottesley et al. 2016). The first two years of life provide a critical window of opportunity for ensuring appropriate growth and development of the child (Singhal et al. 2013; Brambilla et al. 2016). Inappropriate nutrition during infancy can also lead to childhood obesity and neurodevelopmental disorders (WHO, 2009; Anjos et al. 2013; Patience, 2014; Symon et al. 2017).

During the first six months of life, breast milk is the only ideal, unequalled nutritional source for the healthy growth of infants (Badham, 2013). It contains carbohydrates, protein, fat, vitamins, minerals, digestive enzymes and hormones (Fig. 1).

Figure 1: Breast Milk Components and Infant Growth

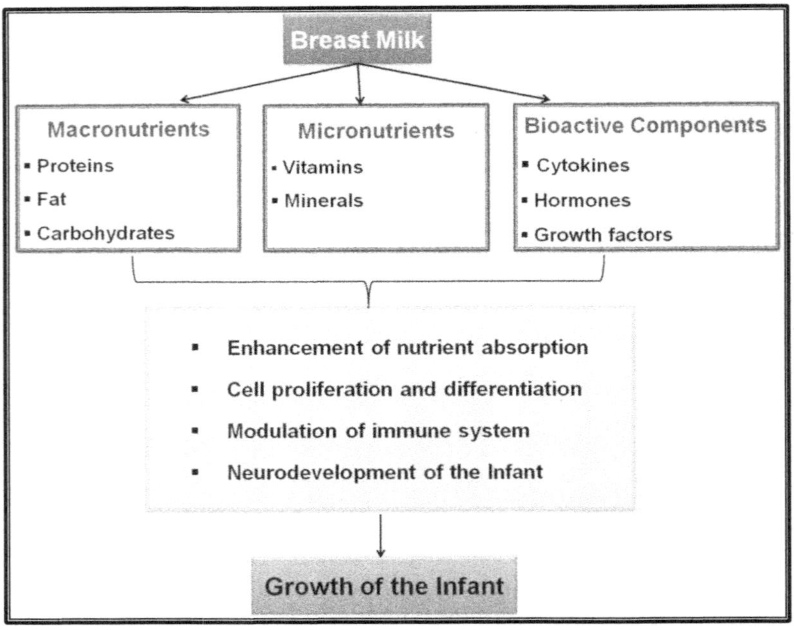

Source: *Demmelmair et al. 2017, Nutrients, 9(8):817*

In addition to these components, it is also rich in immune cells, including macrophages, stem cells and other bioactive components like cytokines, hormones and growth factors (Martin et al. 2016). These nutrients and other bioactive components are known to modify the function of the gastrointestinal tract, immune system and brain development of the infant (Ballard and Morrow, 2013; Demmelmair et al. 2017).

The World Health Organization (WHO) and United Nations Children's Fund (UNICEF) jointly developed the global strategy for exclusive breastfeeding during the first six months of life (WHO and UNICEF, 2003). Breastfeeding is known to reduce morbidity and improve physical and cognitive development of the children (Isaacs et al. 2010; Sankar et al. 2015). Accumulating evidence suggests that breastfeeding reduces the risk of developing obesity, diabetes and cardiovascular disease (CVD) in adulthood (Martin et al. 2005; Yan et al. 2014; Morris, 2018).

1.2 Factors Affecting Breast Milk Composition

Breast milk composition is affected by maternal factors like age, diet, body mass index, parity, smoking, illness, anxiety, stress and mode of delivery (Hoppu et al. 2012; Khodayar-Pardo et al. 2014; Fields et al. 2016) (Fig. 2).

Figure 2: Factors Affecting Breast Milk Composition

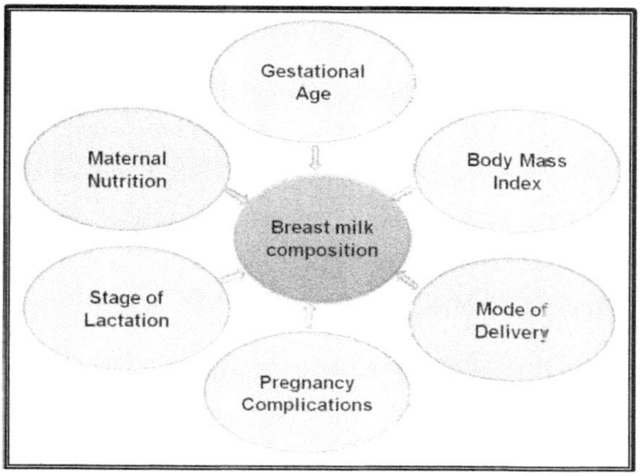

***Source**: Fields et al. 2016, Obesity, 24(6): 1213-1221*

Recent studies indicate that the stage of lactation and pregnancy complications influence the composition of breast milk (Sundekilde et al. 2016; Zambruni et al. 2017) and are discussed below.

1.2.1 Stage of Lactation

Milk composition is known to change over the course of lactation (Ballard and Morrow, 2013). The concentration of several milk metabolites varies significantly in the colostrum, transitional and mature milk (Sundekilde et al. 2016). As lactation progresses, an increase in the concentration of lactose, lipids, calories and phosphate while a decrease in the protein content has been reported (Bauer and Gerss, 2011; Hsu et al. 2014). Fatty acid composition in breast milk is also reported to vary across lactation (Wu et al. 2010). In contrast, milk bioactive components like brain derived neurotrophic factor (BDNF) are reported to be similar up to 90 days of lactation (Li et al. 2011). Adiponectin, epidermal growth factor (EGF) and its receptor, transforming growth factor beta 2 (TGF-β) levels have been shown to increase across lactation in rhesus macaques (Bernstein and Hinde, 2016). The stage of lactation is also shown to influence the cytokine pattern of milk. Interleukin 1 beta (IL-1β), tumor necrosis factor-alpha (TNF-α) and interleukin 6 (IL-6) were shown to be higher at the beginning of lactation in goat milk (Albenzio et al. 2016).

1.2.2 Pregnancy Complications

Pregnancy complications such as gestational diabetes mellitus (GDM), pregnancy induced hypertension (PIH) and preeclampsia are known to affect lactogenesis (Chapman, 2014; Demirci et al. 2018). Studies have reported an increase in glucose levels in the breast milk of diabetic mothers (Plagemann et al. 2002; Whitmore et al. 2012). Further, higher concentration of omega 6 fatty acids has also been reported in the colostrum of women with gestational diabetes mellitus (Azulay Chertok et al. 2017).

Total peroxide and oxidative stress index was shown to be higher in the milk of hypertensive pregnant women as compared to normotensive pregnant women (Erdem et al. 2012). Interleukin 8 (IL-8) and TNF- α levels are also reported to be higher in the mature milk in women with preeclampsia compared to controls indicating an imbalance in oxidative stress and cytokines (Erbagci et al. 2005). Higher levels of pro-inflammatory cytokines and lower levels of anti-inflammatory cytokines have been reported in the milk of women with preeclampsia as compared to normotensive women (Freitas et al. 2018). Increase in immunological components (IgA and IgM) and inflammatory mediators (IFN-γ, TGF-β) have been reported in the colostrum and mature milk of hypertensive mothers (Massmann et al. 2014). Lower levels of adrenomedullin (a potent vasodilator) were observed in the breast milk of women with preeclampsia as compared with normal pregnant women suggesting that it may increase the risk of infection in children (Cekmen et al. 2004).

1.3 Effect of Breastfeeding on Brain Development of Infant

Several studies report a positive association between breastfeeding and neurodevelopment of the infant (Tozzi et al. 2012; McCrory and Murray, 2013). Breastfeeding in the first 28 days of life has been shown to be associated with better intelligence quotient (IQ), working memory and motor function at 7 yrs of age in very preterm infants (Belfort et al. 2016). Similarly, longer breastfeeding duration is reported to be associated with better cognitive and motor development in 2 and 3 yr old children (Bernard et al. 2013).

Studies also report an association between breastfeeding and increased white matter volume, parietal cortex and greater cortical thickness (Isaacs et al. 2010; Kafouri et al. 2013; Deoni et al. 2013; Ou et al. 2014). It is shown that the nervous system of breastfed infants matures earlier than formula fed infants (Khedr et al. 2004). Based on these studies, it can be said that breastfeeding influences brain growth and neuromotor development of the babies. It is believed that the breast milk components play a critical role in the cognitive performance of breastfed children (Isaacs et al. 2010; Guxens et al. 2011). The next section describes the components in milk which influence brain development in children.

1.4 Components of Breast Milk and Brain Development in Children

It is known that breast milk provides most of the nutrients required for the development of the infant brain. Human milk is suggested to improve cognition by providing vital nutrients like fatty acids, choline, amino acids, lactose and trophic factors to the infant and is shown in Fig. 3 (Huppi 2008; Cheatham et al. 2015; Agostoni and Bettocchi, 2016).

Figure 3: Components of Breast Milk and Brain Development in Children

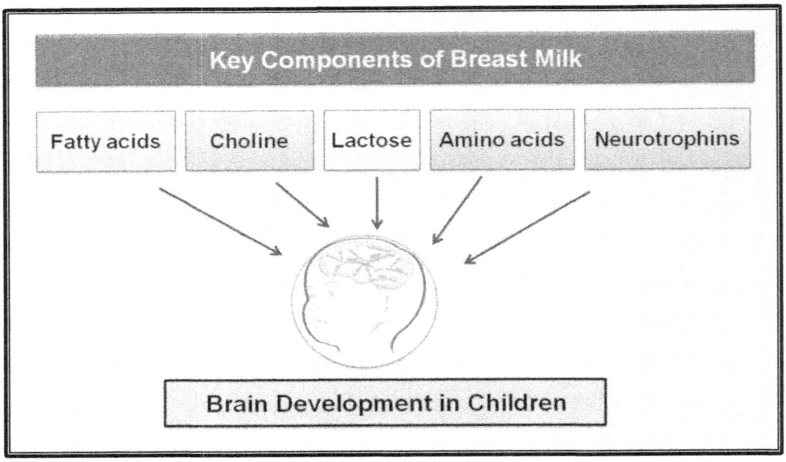

1.4.1 Milk Fatty Acids and Brain Development in Children

Human milk contains 3-5 % of total fat. It is the main source of energy for the newborn. Essential fatty acids (EFA) are the integral part of cell membranes and play a main role in mental and visual development. Two fatty acids are essential for humans: alpha-linolenic acid (ALA, an omega 3 fatty acid) and linoleic acid (LA, an omega 6 fatty acid). They are found in breast milk and serve as precursors for long chain polyunsaturated fatty acids (LCPUFA) like docosahexaenoic acid (DHA) and arachidonic acid (AA) respectively. These fatty acids are essential for normal brain development and are involved in many neurobiological processes like learning and memory (Agostoni et al. 2009; Parletta et al. 2013; Agostoni and Bettocchi, 2016). Many studies have shown that polyunsaturated fatty acid (PUFA) levels in the colostrum are associated with IQ in children up to 6 yr of age (Bernard et al. 2015; Bernard et al. 2017). High content of DHA, in breast milk is reported to be associated with better school performance at 12 yrs of age (Dalmeijer et al. 2016). In contrast, high levels of LA in the colostrum were negatively associated with motor and cognitive scores at 2 and 3 yr of age (Bernard et al. 2015). In contrast, one study reported, no effect of DHA supplementation to lactating mothers on neurodevelopmental outcomes in children (Jensen et al. 2005).

1.4.2 Milk Amino Acids and Brain Development in Children

Amino acids in breast milk are believed to support growth of the infant during the first months of life (Garcia-Rodenas et al. 2016). Glutamate and glutamine are the most abundant free amino acids in human milk (Agostoni et al. 2000). A number of amino acids like glutamate, glutamine and glycine, are recognized as precursors of neurotransmitters that play a key role in long-term potentiation, synaptic plasticity and are important for cognitive functions like learning and memory (Tanaka, 2013; Huang et al. 2017).

1.4.3 Milk Choline and Brain Development in Children

Milk contains a high concentration of choline, phosphocholine and glycerophosphocholine (Ilcol et al. 2005; Ozarda et al. 2014; Wu et al. 2016). Phosphocholine and glycerophosphocholine are storage forms of choline (Zeisel, 2006). Choline is important for the synthesis of membrane phospholipids, specifically phosphatidylcholine. Phosphatidylcholine is the predominant phospholipid in membranes and is critical for maintaining cell structure (Zeisel, 2006). Choline can also be found in sphingomyelin, another membrane phospholipid formed from phosphatidylcholine. Choline is a precursor of acetylcholine, which is a neurotransmitter and is required for lifelong memory function (Zeisel, 2006; Biswas and Giri, 2015). Choline supplementation during pregnancy is reported to improve memory in infants at 6 to 12 mo (Kable et al. 2015).

1.4.4 Milk Lactose and Brain Development in Children

Lactose, a major component of human milk acts as an osmotic agent and contributes to 7% of weight of the milk. It provides energy for the growth of the infants. Human milk contains higher quantity of lactose compared with milk of other species in order to meet high energy demands of the human brain (Andreas et al. 2015). The body breaks it down into two simpler sugars, glucose and galactose. Galactose is a valuable nutrient for brain tissue development (Coelho et al. 2015). However, there is limited literature on role of breast milk lactose and cognitive performance in children.

1.4.5 Milk Neurotrophins and Brain Development in Children

Neurotrophins are a heterogeneous group of proteins which play a crucial role in the development of the central nervous system (CNS) and in the postnatal development of the enteric nervous system (Fichter et al. 2011). There are a variety of neurotrophic factors that have been identified like nerve growth factor (NGF), brain-derived neurotrophic factor (BDNF), insulin-like growth factor (IGF), glial cell-line-derived neurotrophic factor (GDNF), ciliary neurotrophic factor (CNTF), neurotrophin-3 (NT-3), neurotrophic factor-4/5 (NT-4/5) and basic fibroblast growth factor (bFGF). Among these, NGF, BDNF and GDNF are found in the breast milk (Li et al. 2011). NGF and BDNF control neuronal apoptosis during brain development and play an important role in neuronal differentiation, survival and growth of neurons and also modulate synaptic plasticity (Siniscalco et al. 2011; Barichello et al. 2013). BDNF is involved in different aspects of learning and memory processing, such as memory persistence and storage (Bekinschtein et al. 2008). NGF is also critical for enhancing memory formation and facilitating hippocampal long-term potentiation (Conner et al. 2009; Choi et al. 2011). These reports show the potential of breast milk components to enhance cognitive development. However, the role of breast milk neurotrophins in improving cognition in children is unclear.

1.5 Genesis of the Thesis

Preeclampsia is a pregnancy specific disorder that is characterized by new onset of hypertension after the 20th week of gestation (ACOG, 2013). It is often accompanied by proteinuria (Townsend et al. 2016). It is associated with significant maternal and neonatal morbidity and mortality (Backes et al. 2011). It affects around 10% of all pregnancies worldwide (ACOG, 2013). In India, the prevalence of preeclampsia is reported to be 8-10% among the pregnant women (National Health Portal, 2016). Pregnancy complications such as preeclampsia and gestational diabetes mellitus have been known to affect lactogenesis (milk production) (Kaushik et al. 2002; Erbagci et al. 2005).

Breast milk contains wide range of nutrients and growth factors which play a vital role in the growth and development of the infant (Jackson et al. 2006; Bertino et al. 2012; Serpero et al. 2012). Milk fatty acids, specifically long chain polyunsaturated fatty acids and growth factors like neurotrophins and hormones influence the cognitive performance of the infant (Yum, 2007). Apart from these components, choline, lactose and amino acids are also required for the neurodevelopment of the infant and are provided through breast milk.

Reports indicate that the milk components change over the course of lactation in a time dependent manner based on the requirement of the child for optimal development (Li et al. 2011; Ballard and Morrow, 2013). Several longitudinal studies have examined variations in milk fatty acids levels in healthy women across lactation (Molnar et al. 2002; Mihalyi et al. 2015; Zhao et al. 2018). A longitudinal study in normotensive women demonstrates that milk BDNF remains same during the period of lactation i.e. from day 3 to 90 day of lactation (Li et al. 2011). It has been suggested that there are significant changes in the human milk metabolome at different stages of lactation. A study reports significant increase in concentrations of milk lactose, choline, alanine, glutamate, and glutamine, as well as decrease in the levels of citrate, phosphocholine, glycerophosphocholine, and N-acetyl glucosamine in healthy women (Wu et al. 2016). Milk levels of valine, leucine, betaine and creatinine are reported to be high in the colostrum as compared to mature milk in mothers delivering at term. Similarly, the levels of glutamate, caprylate and caprate were shown to increase in mature term milk compared with colostrum (Sundekilde et al. 2016). However, these studies were carried out on a small sample size.

An earlier cross-sectional study carried out in our department demonstrated higher milk DHA levels at day 3 of lactation in women with preeclampsia (Dangat et al. 2010). Therefore, it is unclear whether the vital constituents such as fatty acids, neurotrophins, amino acids, choline and lactose remain altered during the complete duration of lactation. To the best of our knowledge, no studies have been carried to examine the levels of fatty acids, neurotrophins and various other metabolites in human milk across the period of lactation in women with preeclampsia. The associations of these milk components with infant growth and cognitive performance is also unclear.

Research indicates that preeclampsia is associated with an increased risk for impaired early language development, lower neurocognitive functioning and attention-deficit hyperactivity disorder in children (ADHD) (Many et al. 2003; Whitehouse et al. 2012; Getahun et al. 2013; Postma et al. 2014). Evidence suggests that hypertension during pregnancy, especially preeclampsia, can have long-term consequences on neurobehavioral development of the offspring (Nomura et al. 2017). It has been reported that maternal hypertensive disorders of pregnancy are a risk factor for reduction in offspring verbal ability (Whitehouse et al. 2012). It has been demonstrated that the babies born to women with preeclampsia are at higher risk of behavior problems (Robinson et al. 2009) and cognitive impairment (Ratsep et al. 2016a) than offspring born to normotensive women. In addition, Walker et al. report that preeclampsia is associated with autism spectrum disorder and developmental delays in children (Walker et al. 2015). Children born to mothers with preeclampsia are reported to have enlarged volumes of cerebellum, temporal lobe, brain stem, and right and left amygdalae in the brain (Ratsep et al. 2016b).

The role of breast milk components in influencing cognitive abilities during infancy and childhood is unclear. In view of this, it is essential to examine the levels of various milk components in women with preeclampsia and their association with cognitive performance in children.

1.6 Hypothesis

"Milk components will be altered in women with preeclampsia and will affect cognitive performance in children"

The present study for the first time simultaneously examines the levels of fatty acids, neurotrophins and other vital metabolites like choline, amino acids and lactose in the breast milk of women with preeclampsia at various time points across lactation. This study also reports the growth and cognitive performance in children at 3-6 yrs of age.

CHAPTER 2
AIM AND OBJECTIVES

2.1 Aim

The present study aims to examine the breast milk components and neurodevelopmental risk in children born to mothers with preeclampsia.

2.2 Objectives

1. To examine the levels of long chain polyunsaturated fatty acids (LCPUFA) and neurotrophins (nerve growth factor and brain derived neurotrophic factor) in breast milk at various time points across lactation in normotensive women and women with preeclampsia.
2. To examine the status of breast milk metabolites (alanine, acetate, acetone, glutamine, gluamate, citrate, creatine, phosphocreatine, choline, phosphocholoine, glycerophosphocholine, glycine, α-lactose and β-lactose) at day 3 and 6 month of lactation in women with preeclampsia and compare them with normotensive women.
3. To compare the cognitive performance of children born to mothers with preeclampsia and children born to normotensive mothers.
4. To examine the associations of milk fatty acids with infant growth and cognitive performance in children.

CHAPTER 3
REVIEW OF LITERATURE

The earlier chapter described the genesis and rationale for the current work. This chapter summarizes various studies which have examined the levels of breast milk components in normotensive women and women with preeclampsia. It also describes studies which report the importance of breastfeeding and neurodevelopment in children.

3.1 Importance of Breast Milk

Early life nutrition is important for the growth and development of the infant. Breast milk provides optimal nutrition for infants during the first six months of life (Lessen and Kavanagh, 2015). Milk is a complex biochemical fluid and it contains 3,000 different components. It also contains bioactive components like growth factors, cytokines and hormones (Savino et al. 2011; Mosca and Gianni, 2017). Human milk nutrients support rapid brain, enteric and immunologic development of neonates (He et al. 2016; Nurliyana et al. 2016; Kumar et al. 2017). Milk bioactive components are required to protect infants against infection and inflammation. They also contribute to healthy microbial colonization of the neonatal intestine, immune maturation and development of various organs (Ballard and Morrow, 2013).

3.2 Global Strategy for Breastfeeding

According to WHO, "Exclusive breastfeeding" is defined as "no other food or drink, not even water, except breast milk" (WHO, 2009). The American Academy of Paediatrics also recommends breastfeeding for at least twelve months (Eidelman, 2012). It has been reported that only 35% of infants worldwide are exclusively breastfed during the first four months of life. The percentage of breastfeeding at twelve months is highest in sub-Saharan Africa, South Asia and in parts of Latin America as shown in Fig. 4 (Victora et al. 2016).The prevalence of exclusive breastfeeding rate globally is reported to be 43% (Suresh et al. 2014). The rate of exclusive breastfeeding continues to be low in India (Dadhich and Agarwal, 2009; Travasso, 2015). In India, according to the National Family Health Survey-4 (NFHS-4), exclusive breastfeeding rate at 6 months was only 55% (NFHS-4, 2015-2016). Most of the infant deaths, which are often associated with inappropriate feeding practices, occur during the first year of life. Studies have demonstrated that breastfeeding reduces deaths in infants and young children (UNICE, Infant and Young Child Feeding programming guide, 2013; Katepa-Bwalya et al. 2015). In 2003, Lancet series on child survival and later Lancet series on newborn survival summarized that globally, 13% of deaths of children under 5 could be prevented if 90% of babies were breastfed exclusively for the first six months and continued to breastfeed for the first year (Jones et al. 2003; Darmstadt et al. 2005).

Figure 4: Global Distribution of Breastfeeding at 12 Months

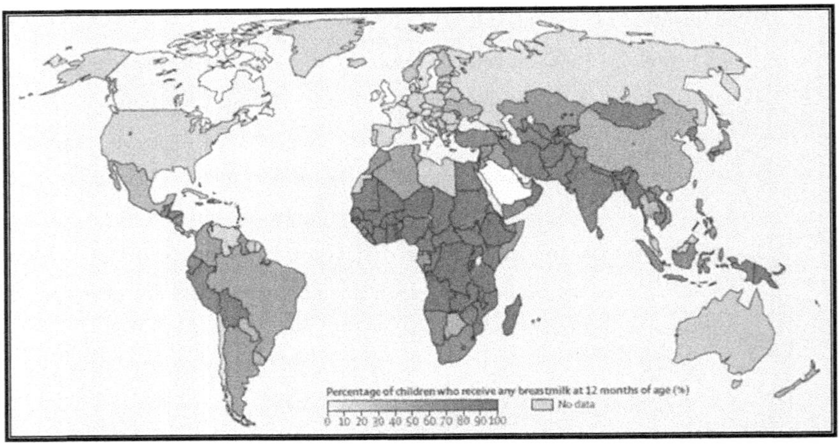

Source: *Victora et al. 2016, Lancet, 387(10017):475-490*

3.2.1 Breastfeeding and Associated Outcomes

It has been shown that breastfeeding is important for both short and long-term health benefits of the children (Fig. 5).

Figure 5: Benefits of Breastfeeding to the Infant

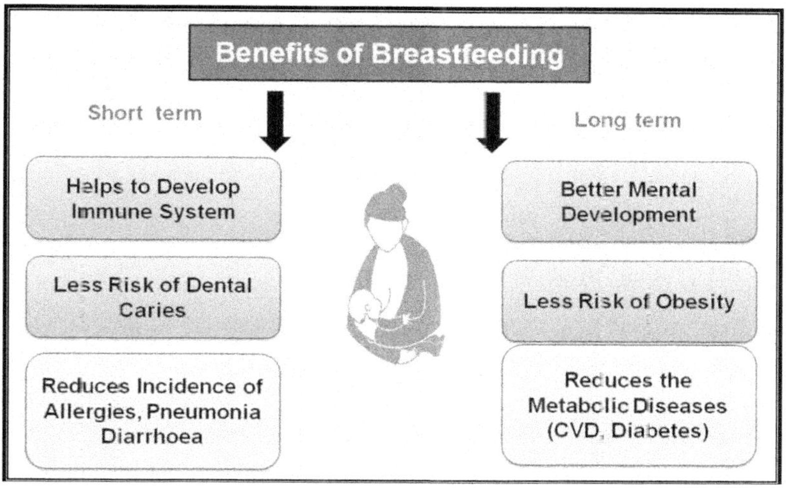

CVD: Cardiovascular Disease

A number of reports have evaluated the impact of breastfeeding on child mortality and morbidity due to infectious diseases in childhood (Sankar et al. 2015; Victora et al. 2016). It has been reported that neonates who are partially breastfed have a higher risk of mortality as compared to exclusively breastfed neonates (Mullany et al. 2008). Lack of breastfeeding has been shown to be associated with elevated risk of pneumonia and diarrhoea in infants and young children (Bener et al. 2011; Lamberti et al. 2013; Santos et al. 2015). A systematic review and meta-analysis showed significant association between exclusive breastfeeding and reduced risk for developing otitis media (infection of the middle ear) (Bowatte et al. 2015). A negative association has been shown between breastfeeding (longer than 12 months) and the occurrence of dental caries (Santos et al. 2016).

Breastfeeding is also shown to influence the development of noncommunicable diseases in childhood and adulthood (Bernardo et al. 2013). It has been suggested that breastfeeding may prevent the development of overweight/obesity, in early life and also in the later life (Papatesta and

Iacovidou, 2013; Yan et al. 2014). A retrospective database study reported that breastfeeding is associated with a reduced risk of diabetes in the offspring (Martens et al. 2016). A short duration of breastfeeding (<40 days) was shown to be associated with increase in blood pressure in school children at 8 yrs of age (Amorim Rde et al. 2014). A longitudinal survey carried out in Japan observed associations between breastfeeding and behavioral development outcomes at age 2.5 and 5.5 yrs (Yorifuji et al. 2014). Long-term breastfeeding has been shown to be associated with higher neuropsychological functions in children at 4 yrs of age (Julvez et al. 2014).

3.3 Anatomy of the Breast

The breast is composed of glandular (secretory) and adipose (fatty) tissues, and is supported by connective fibres called Cooper's ligaments that form the structural framework of the breast (Jesinger, 2014). The glandular tissue is composed of lobes, which are comprised of lobules containing groups of alveoli (Geddes, 2007). Alveoli are the basic components of a mature mammary gland (hollow cavities, a few millimeters large) lined with milk-secreting cuboidal cells and surrounded by myoepithelial cells. These alveoli join to form groups known as lobules (Macias and Hinck, 2012) as shown in Fig. 6.

Figure 6: Structure of Mammary gland

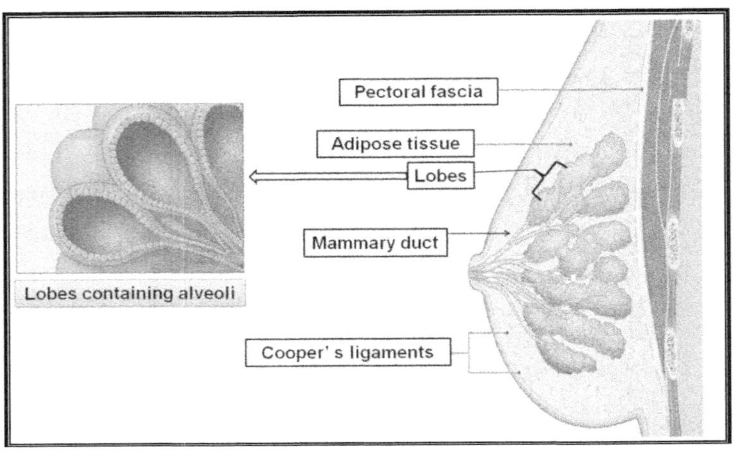

Source: *Anatomy and Physiology of the Breast ID: 11014009*

Each lobule has a lactiferous duct that drains into openings in the nipple (Zucca-Matthes et al. 2016). These small ducts join to form larger ducts and larger ducts finally merge into one milk duct for each lobe. Infant suckling stimulates the nerve endings in the nipple and areola, which signal the pituitary gland in the brain to release two hormones, prolactin and oxytocin (Jonas et al. 2009). Prolactin is the main factor regulating milk production through osmotic balance. Oxytocin is transported in the maternal bloodstream to the mammary gland, causing alveoli to contract and eject milk (Gardner et al. 2015).

3.4 Lactogenesis

The breast undergoes massive anatomical changes due to the action of certain hormones during pregnancy, to attain its full functional capacity to synthesize milk constituents. The process of initiation of lactation (lactogenesis) occurs in two phases: lactogenesis I and lactogenesis II (Czank et al., 2007; Pang and Hartmann, 2007). Lactogenesis I is the first stage of lactogenesis beginning at about sixteen weeks of pregnancy. The hormone prolactin is necessary for the development of the alveolar glands. This stage of lactatogenesis will extend through delivery to the first few days of postpartum (Brown, 2010). Lactogenesis II is the second stage of lactogenesis that occurs two to five days after giving birth.

Breast milk has three different and distinct stages: colostrum, transitional milk and mature milk.

Colostrum

Colostrum is the first stage of breast milk and lasts for several days after the birth of the baby. Colostrum is rich in proteins, fat-soluble vitamins, minerals and immunoglobulins.

Transitional milk

Transitional milk occurs after colostrum and lasts for approximately two weeks. Transitional milk contains high levels of fat, lactose and water-soluble vitamins. It contains more calories than colostrum.

Mature milk

Mature milk is the final milk that is produced and 90% of it is water. The other 10% is composed of carbohydrates, proteins, and fats which are necessary for both growth and energy.

Further, breast milk it is often described as having two parts, foremilk and hindmilk. Foremilk is the milk released at the start of a feeding and hindmilk is the milk released at the end.

3.5 Breast Milk Composition

Human breast milk is a complex matrix with a composition of 87% water, 3.8% fat, 1 % protein, and 7% lactose. However, milk composition varies during lactation according to needs of the growing child (Martin et al. 2016).

3.5.1 Fats

Fat is one of the crucial nutrients out of three main macronutrients (carbohydrate protein and fat) that provide energy. This is the most variable component of human milk (Ballard and Morrow, 2013). The fat fraction of human milk is composed of several different classes of lipids. More than 98% of the total milk fat is in the form of triacylglycerols and small amounts of di- and monoacylgylcerols, nonesterified fatty acids, phospholipids, cholesterol and cholesterol esters (Giuffrida et al. 2013; Michalski, 2013). The triacylglycerols are hydrolyzed to free fatty acids and glycerol by the action of lipase present both in infant gut and in human milk.

Fatty Acids

Fatty acids (FAs) are major components of triglycerols and phospholipids. Fatty acids are membrane constituents and serve as energy source (Wakil and Abu-Elheiga, 2009). They are mainly involved in the regulation of membrane structure and function; regulation of intracellular signalling pathways, transcription factor activity, and gene expression; and regulation of the production of bioactive lipid mediators (Calder, 2015).

FAs are composed of large chain of carbon atoms bonded with hydrogen atoms as shown in Fig. 7. Most naturally occurring fatty acids have a chain of 4 to 28 carbons. At one of the terminal ends of a fatty acid, is a carboxyl group (-COOH), which is the reactive portion of the molecule that participates in chemical reactions to make lipids and to store energy.

Figure 7: Structure of a Fatty Acid (e.g. Palmitic acid; C16:0)

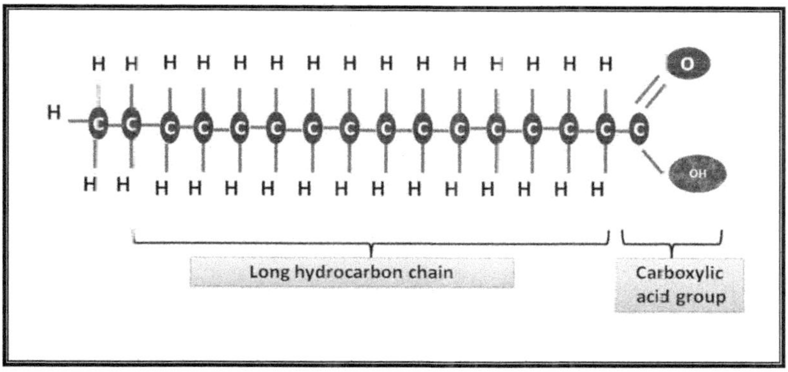

FAs are classified according to the presence of double bonds in the carbon chain such as saturated fatty acids (that possess no double bonds) and unsaturated fatty acids (that possess double bonds). Unsaturated fatty acids are further classified into monounsaturated fatty acids (i.e. MUFA; 1 double bond) and polyunsaturated fatty acids (i.e. PUFA; >1 double bond) (Fig. 8).

Breast milk, contains 214 different fatty acids (Jensen, 1999), however, many of these are present in very low concentrations and they arise from three different origins: from the maternal body store mobilization, from the mammary gland and from diet (Rodríguez-Cruz et al. 2009; Rodriguez-Cruz et al. 2011). In human milk, saturated fatty acid content ranges from 20% to 70% of total fatty acid, MUFA from 23% to 55%, PUFA from 6% to 36%, and long chain polyunsaturated fatty acid (LCPUFA) from 0.3% to 8% (Giuffrida et al. 2016). Fatty acids like, oleic, palmitic and linoleic acid are found in the highest concentrations in breast milk (Andreas et al. 2015).

Figure 8: Types of Fatty Acids

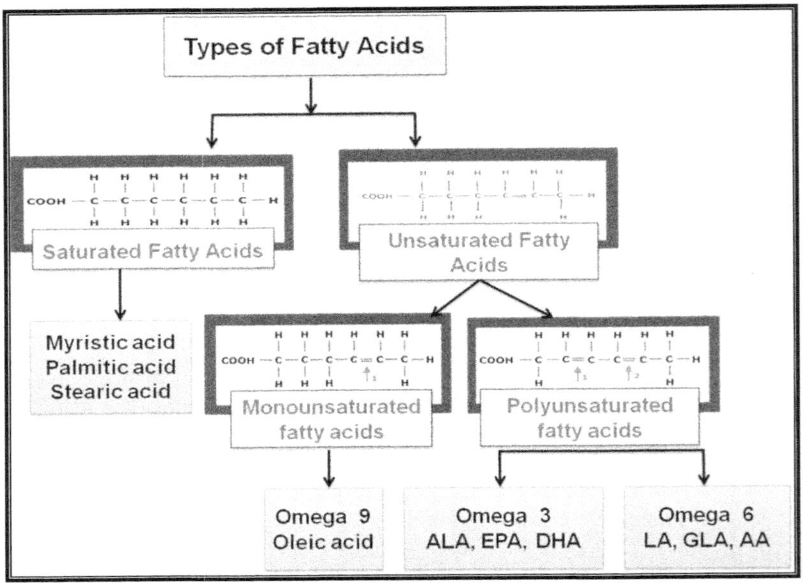

ALA: Alpha-linolenic; **EPA:** Eicosapentaenoic acid; **DHA**: Docosahexaenoic acid**; LA:** Linoleic acid; **GLA:** Gamma-linolenic acid; **AA:** Arachidonic acid

Saturated Fatty Acids

Saturated Fatty Acids (SFAs) act as a source of energy and they also play metabolic and structural roles. The most common SFAs in infant nutrition have 12-, 14-, 16- and 18-carbon chains. Palmitic acid is an important component of breast milk; it accounts for approximately 25% of fatty acids in its composition (González and Visentin, 2016).

Essential Fatty Acids

Essential Fatty Acids (EFAs) are required by the body, but cannot be synthesized in the body because humans lack the desaturase enzymes required for their production and therefore must be obtained from the food. In the body, EFAs regulate a wide range of functions, including blood pressure, blood clotting, lipid levels, immune response, and the inflammation response to injury infections.

Only two fatty acids are known to be essential for humans: alpha-linolenic (ALA) acid and linoleic acid (LA).

Long Chain Polyunsaturated Fatty Acids (LCPUFA)

EFA are the parent compounds of the LCPUFA. There are two series of LCPUFA i.e. Omega 3 and omega 6 fatty acid series. Omega 3 and 6 are named based on the position of the first double bond from the methyl end in a fatty acid chain. Omega 3 fatty acids with the first double bond on the third carbon and omega 6 fatty acids with the first double bond on the sixth carbon (Lee et al. 2016).

Omega 3 fatty acids include ALA, eicosapentaenoic acid (EPA), and docosahexaenoic acid (DHA). They are components of brain cell membranes and retina. They influence membrane fluidity and regulate membrane-receptor functions DHA is also a precursor of anti-inflammatory and immunoregulatory docosanoids such as resolvins and protectins (Duvall and Levy, 2016). The main dietary sources for ALA are canola, flaxseed, linseed and rapeseed oils, walnuts, and green leafy vegetables. The major source of EPA and DHA in the diet is from marine fish.

Omega 6 fatty acids include LA, gamma-linolenic acid (GLA), dihomo-gamma-linolenic acid (DGLA) and arachidonic acid (AA). Omega 6 fatty acids play a vital role in many physiological functions. AA is involved in several pathways and is a precursor of anti-inflammatory eicosanoids (Fleith and Clandinin, 2005; Innis, 2007). Sources of LA include cereals, eggs, most vegetable oils (safflower and groundnut oil), whole-grain breads, and margarine (Ollis et al. 1999; Das, 2002). GLA is also found in some fungal sources (Horrobin, 1983; Ollis et al. 1999). AA is found in meat, egg yolks, some seaweeds, and dairy products.

PUFA Synthesis

The principal pathway for PUFA synthesis involves desaturation and elongation. Same desaturation/elongation pathway is used in omega 3 and omega 6 fatty acid synthesis (Burdge and Calder, 2005) (Fig. 9). The process of elongation adds more carbon atoms to the fatty acid, while desaturation involves addition of double bonds to the carboxyl end of fatty acid molecules. These processes use some specific enzymes called "desaturases" for synthesizing LCPUFA, such as delta 6 (Δ6), Δ5 and Δ4 desaturase and elongase. Δ6 and Δ4-desaturase can generate both omega 6 and omega 3 fatty acids. Δ5 and Δ6 desaturase catalyze the desaturation of fatty acids at specific positions (Vrablik and Watts, 2012). Stearoyl-CoA desaturase (SCD) also called Δ9 desaturase. SCD is the main enzyme responsible for converting saturated fatty acids into monounsaturated fatty acids (Sjogren et al. 2008). They are mainly present in liver cell endoplasmic reticulum (Rodriguez et al. 1998). Δ9 deasturase is used to produce the monounsaturated fatty acid i.e oleic acid from the saturated fatty acid i.e stearic acid (Flowers and Ntambi, 2008). In the body, the conversion of LA and ALA to gamma-linolenic acid (GLA; 18:3) and stearidonic acid (18:4) is determined by the enzymatic activity of Δ6 desaturase (Rodriguez-Cruz et al. 2006). The Δ5 desaturase introduces another double bond at the Δ-5 position of dihomo-gamma-linolenic acid (DGLA; 20:3) and eicosatetraenoic acid (ETA; 20:4) to synthesize AA and EPA, respectively. Further, Δ-6 desaturase is also required for the synthesis of DHA from EPA.

Figure 9: Biosynthesis of Polyunsaturated Fatty Acids

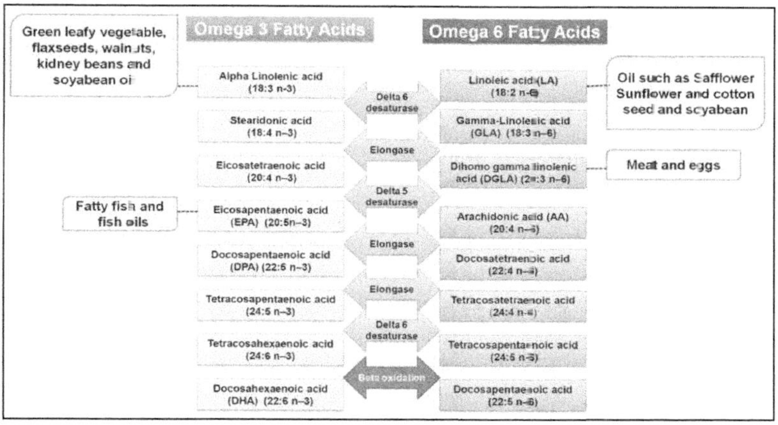

Source: *De Caterina and Raffaele, 2011, N Engl J Me, 364(25): 2439-2450*

3.5.2 Carbohydrates

Human milk is rich in carbohydrates. Lactose and oligosaccharides are the major components of milk representing approximately 6.8 and 1% of the milk, respectively (Newburg, 2013). Human milk also contains monosaccharides (mainly glucose and galactose) and more than 130 different oligosaccharides in lower concentrations (German et al. 2008).

Lactose is composed of glucose and galactose linked together by 1, 4 β-glycosidic bond, and is synthesized in the golgi secretory vesicle system of lactocytes. Lactose content in breast milk is 7.2g/100ml and it acts as a main energy source for neonates (Liu et al. 2016). In addition to providing energy, lactose is the osmotically active component of human milk. Lactose is a source of galactose which is essential for the production of galactolipids. These galactolipids are essential for the CNS development (Varma et al. 1962). Lactose is synthesized in the endoplasmic reticulum of mammary gland (Kresge and Simoni, 2006).

Human milk oligosaccharides (HMO) are an important component of human milk carbohydrate and are the third largest component in breast milk, with an average 12.9 g/L in mature milk and 20.9 g/L at 4 days post-partum (Coppa et al. 1993). There are over 200 different types of oligosaccharides in human milk (German et al. 2008). HMO function as prebiotics, encouraging the growth of certain strains of beneficial bacteria, such as *Bifidobacterium infantis*, within the infant gastrointestinal tract, protecting the infant from colonization by pathogenic bacteria (Ward et al. 2006). HMO plays an important role in preventing neonatal diarrheal and respiratory tract infections.

3.5.3 Protein

Human milk contains over 400 different proteins which perform a variety of functions (Molinari et al. 2012). They provide nutrition to the infant, help in digestion, protect against pathogens and help promote healthy gut microbiota (Lönnerdal et al. 2003). The majority of breast milk proteins not synthesized by lactocytes (milk-producing cell in the mammary epithelium) are taken up from the maternal circulation via transcytosis, passing into the lumen (Neville, 1983). Proteins in milk also make up the immune factors and hormones.

Milk proteins are classified into three groups: milk fat globule membrane proteins, casein and whey proteins. Whey fraction constitutes the major part of protein (~60-70%), whereas casein is a smaller fraction (~30-40%) (Lönnerdal, 2003; Liao et al. 2011). The majority of milk proteins including caseins and several whey proteins (lactoferrin, α-lactalbumin, whey acidic proteins) are synthesized by lactocytes by the endoplasmic reticulum from free amino acids. After synthesis they are packaged into golgi secretory vesicles and secreted into milk by exocytosis (Neville, 1983). Protein content decreases significantly from day 1 to 3 at week 10 to 12 as lactation progresses (Mimouni et al. 2017). Proteins in human milk provide an important source of amino acids to the rapidly growing infants (Lönnerdal, 2003). Milk amino acid content is known to change as infants mature due to changes in the amino acid content of whey proteins and casein.

Amino acids can be divided into indispensable and dispensable. Indispensable amino acids are histidine, isoleucine, leucine, lysine, methionine, phenylalanine, threonine, valine and dispensable amino acids are alanine, argentine, aspartic acid asparagines, cystine, glutamic acid, glutamine, glycine, proline, serine and tyrosine (Garcia-Rodenas et al. 2016). Taurine, glutamic acid, and glutamine are the most abundant free amino acids in human milk. Glutamine is important for providing ketoglutaric acid for the citric acid cycle. It acts as a neurotransmitter in the brain and serves as a major energy substrate for intestinal cells (Agostoni et al. 2000). Glutamine is synthesized from glutamate. Free glutamine is abundant in human milk but is found in much lower concentrations in formula. Glutamine is nearly 20 times higher in mature milk than the colostrum (Zhang et al. 2013).

Glutamate is a nonessential amino acid. Adequate amounts of glutamate and glycine are critical for glutathione synthesis. Glycine is required for the synthesis of proteins, porphyrins, nucleotides, creatine, and glutathione. Glycine is an inhibitory neurotrasmitter required for infant brain development. Glycine is present in small amounts in human milk as it is also essential for the synthesis of glutathione (the major intracellular antioxidant).

3.5.4 Choline

Choline is a dietary component essential for the normal function of all the cells (Zeisel, 2004). Choline and its metabolites give structural integrity and perform signalling functions of cell membranes. It is important for liver function, normal brain development, nerve function, and muscle movement (Zeisel, 2006; Michel et al. 2011). It acts as a source of the methyl a group which is used for the production of phosphatidylcholine in the N-methyltransferase phosphatidylethanolamine (PEMT) pathway (Yan et al. 2012). It is also important for the functioning of a key neurotransmitter called acetylcholine, which helps nerves to communicate (Zeisel, 2012). Choline is actively transported from the mother to fetus across the placenta and from mother to infant through the breast milk. Choline in milk can be derived from active uptake from maternal circulation and from *de novo* synthesis within the mammary gland (Garcia-Rodenas et al. 2016). Phosphocholine and glycerophosphocholine are storage forms for choline (Zeisel, 2006). The total choline concentration in milk ranges from 1.35 to 1.60 mmol/L (144–170 mg/L). In human milk, the majority of choline is found as phosphocholine and glycerophosphocholine (Wiedeman and Whitfield, 2018). It is reported that higher milk choline is related to better recognition memory (Cheatham and Sheppard, 2015).

3.5.5 Vitamins and Minerals

Human breast milk provides all the vitamins and essential minerals that are required for the growth of infant (Martin et al. 2016). Fat-soluble (A, D, E) and water-soluble vitamins (vitamin C, riboflavin, niacin, and pantothenic acid) are vital for the health of the infant. All the vitamins, except K, are found in human milk in significant concentrations. The amount and types of vitamins in breast milk are related to the mother's vitamin intake.

The principal mineral constituents of human milk are Na, K, Ca, Mg, P, and Cl (Parr et al. 1991). Calcium and phosphorus concentrations vary from 25-35 mg/100 ml and 13-16 mg/100 ml respectively (Jenness, 1979). Iron, copper and zinc contents of human milk vary considerably i.e Copper content in milk gradually decreases from 0.38 mg/L to 0.19 mg/L by the 90th day of lactation and zinc concentration decreases sharply from 7.99 to 3.3 mg/L. Iron content in milk varies from 0.56 to 0.40 mg/L by the 30th day of lactation (Silvestre et al. 2001). Maternal thiamin, riboflavin, vitamin B_6, vitamin B_{12}, choline, retinol, vitamin A, vitamin D, selenium, and iodine deficiency can result in very low concentrations of these vitamins in milk. Folate, calcium, iron, copper, and zinc in breast milk is relatively unaffected by maternal intake (Allen, 2012).

3.5.6 Other Bioactive Factors

Human milk provides different types and classes of bioactive factors, such as enzymes, hormones, and growth factors, many of which have a role in supporting infantile growth and development. The bioactive agents include antimicrobial factors (e.g. secretory IgA, oligosaccharides), anti-inflammatory agents and transporters (e.g. lactoferrin) and digestive enzymes (e.g. bile salt-stimulated lipase (BSSL)). Several nonpeptide hormones (thyroid hormones, cortisol, progesterone, pregnanediol and estrogens) and peptide hormones and growth factors (erythropoietin, epidermal growth factor (EGF) insulin, insulin-like growth factor-I, nerve growth factor (NGF), brain-derived neurotrophic factor (BDNF), transforming growth factor-alpha (TGF-alpha), gastrointestinal regulatory peptides and thyroid-parathyroid hormones) have been isolated and quantitated in human milk (Clarke and May, 2000; Gregory and Walker, 2013;

Velasco et al. 2016). These growth modulators are produced either by the epithelial cells of the mammary gland or by activated macrophages, lymphocytes (mainly T cells), or neutrophils in the milk. EGF and TGF-alpha were found at higher concentrations in the milk of mothers who delivered prematurely compared with those who delivered at term (Castellote et al. 2011). Higher expression of neurotrophic factors (BDNF, Glial cell-derived neurotrophic factor, Neurotrophin-3) have been observed in the mature preterm milk samples as compared to the mature term samples (Collado et al. 2015). It is also reported that the milk ghrelin and leptin levels are higher at 2 months of lactation and there was a positive correlation between the breast milk IGF-1 level and infant weight gain (Kon et al. 2014). Some biologically active proteins like lysozyme, lactoferrin, leptin, adiponectin and β-endorphin decrease while there is no change in secretory immunoglobulin A (sIgA) during the first month of lactation in both term and preterm breast milk samples (Mehta and Petrova, 2011). Similarly, the concentrations of milk interleukin (IL)-10 and IL-12 decreases as the lactation progresses (Yilmaz et al. 2007).

3.5.7 Neurotrophins

Neurotrophins are a heterogeneous group of proteins and peptides which play crucial roles in the developing central nervous system (CNS) and in the postnatal development of the enteric nervous system (ENS) (Fichter et al. 2011). These include nerve growth Factor (NGF), brain-derived neurotrophic factor (BDNF), insulin-like growth factor (IGF), Glial cell-line-derived neurotrophic factor (GDNF), ciliary neurotrophic factor (CNTF), Neurotrophin-3 (NT-3), neurotrophic factor-4/5 (NT-4/5), basic fibroblast growth factor (bFGF). Among these factors, NGF, BDNF and GDNF are found in the breast milk (Wani et al. 2017; Li et al. 2011). Neurotrophins are synthesized as precursor forms (proneurotrophins). Mature forms of neurotrophins exert their effect by binding to specific tropomyosin kinase receptor (TrkA, TrkB and TrkC) as well as via the p75 receptor (Bartkowska et al. 2010) as shown in Fig. 10.

Figure 10: Neurotrophins and Their Receptors

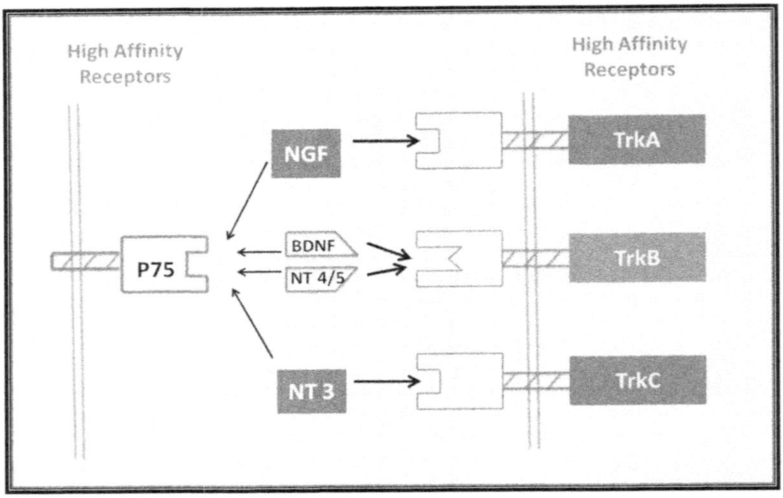

Source: *Ghanbarzadeh et al. 2016, Ann Mil Health Sci Res, 14(4):e59774*

Neurotrophins are secreted by developing organs. Evidence demonstrates that mammary cells also synthesize neurotrophins. Hassiotou et al. demonstrated an upregulation of pro-NGF and downregulation of NT-3 and p75NTR in the lactating breast (Hassiotou et al. 2014).

Brain-Derived Neurotrophic Factor

Brain-derived neurotrophic factor (BDNF) is a small dimeric neuroprotective protein belonging to the neurotrophin family (Liong, 2015). BDNF mediates neuronal plasticity, migration and survival in both the central and peripheral nervous system (Ghanbarzadeh et al. 2016; Lin et al. 2016). Additionally, BDNF plays a crucial role in learning and memory processing (Bekinschtein et al. 2008). Apart from neuron and glial cells, BDNF is also present in mucosal cells of the colon and is involved in the control of colonic peristalsis (constriction and relaxation of the muscles of the intestine) (Boesmans et al. 2008). BDNF binds to two receptors on the surface of cells that include high affinity tropomyosin kinase receptor B (TrkB) and the low affinity receptor p75 (De la Cruz-Morcillo et al. 2016). A number of neurodevelopmental disorders like bipolar disorder, schizophrenia, attention-deficit hyperactivity disorder (ADHD) have been associated with lower levels of BDNF (Hashimoto et al. 2005; Corominas-Roso et al. 2013; Li et al. 2014).

There are only few studies which demonstrate that BDNF is present in mature human milk (Li et al. 2011; Ismail et al. 2015). There is no evidence that BDNF in human milk is derived entirely from the serum or mammary gland cells (Li et al. 2011). However, it is reported that human milk contains leukocytes expressing BDNF (Enstrom et al. 2008). There is a report which indicates no change in milk BDNF levels at days 3, 10, 30, and 90 after parturition in Chinese women (Li et al. 2011).

Nerve Growth Factor

Nerve growth factor (NGF) is a family of proteins that induces survival, proliferation, differentiation, and neuroprotective effects on sensory, sympathetic, and certain cholinergic neurons in the nervous system (Dreyfus, 1989; Sofroniew et al. 2001; Xiao and Le, 2016). NGF initiates biological functions by interacting with its associated receptors tropomyosin kinase receptor A (TrkA). NGF plays a crucial role in the process of angiogenesis (Ahluwalia et al. 2016) and cell development as well as tissue proliferation in the brain (De Nicoló et al. 2013).

NGF is present in human milk (Wright and Gaull, 1983; Wani et al. 2017). An animal study showed that during the period of early lactation, bioactive NGF is present in mouse milk, but sources are not known (Grueters et al. 1985).

3.6 Factors Influencing Human Milk

Variation of breast milk composition is known to affect the infant's health, growth, and development. Milk composition is influenced by many parameters such as maternal, physiological, environmental and psychological factors. Maternal factors that affect milk composition include age, diet, parity, mode of delivery, pregnancy complications, body mass index, smoking, illness, anxiety and stress, gestational age and suckling ability of infant (Dewey, 2001; Zanardo et al. 2005).

Maternal Nutrition

Maternal nutrition during pregnancy and lactation is important for the well being of the infants. Nutritional requirements are higher in infancy as compared to other stages of development. Maternal nutrition has major impact on breast milk composition (Bravi et al. 2016). It can influence human milk composition in three ways: current dietary intake, nutrient stores in the body and alterations in nutrient utilization. The nutritional needs of the fetus depend on the intake of nutrients of the mother, their metabolism, and their distribution through maternal circulation and on the placental transport mechanism (Castrogiovanni and Imbesi, 2017).

It is reported that maternal protein (Nommsen et al. 1991) and carbohydrate intake (Nikniaz et al. 2009) is positively associated with lipid concentrations in the milk. Further, maternal fat intake is also reported to influence lactoferrin concentrations in the breast milk (Leelahakul et al. 2009). Many micronutrients including vitamins and trace elements vary in human milk depending on the maternal diet and body stores. Poor maternal intake of thiamin, riboflavin, vitamin B_6, B_{12} and choline, is shown to result into reduced concentrations of these nutrients in the breast milk (Allen, 2012). Some studies showed a positive correlation between dietary intake of vitamin C, B_{12}, B_1 and its concentration in breast milk (Ortega et al. 2004; Hoppu et al; 2005; Deegan et al. 2011). Levels of calcium and copper in milk are also influenced by dietary intake of calcium and copper (Maru et al. 2013). In contrast, a cross sectional study, found that there is no association between dietary intake of vitamin E and its concentration in breast milk (Martysiak-Zurowska et al. 2013). Dietary intake of zinc, copper, and iron during pregnancy had no effect on its concentrations in milk (Nakamori et al. 2009). It has been shown that the pattern of fatty acids in the maternal diet alters the fatty acid composition of the milk (Jiang et al. 2016; Kim et al. 2017).

Maternal Age

Higher maternal age at delivery is common but little is known regarding the effect of maternal age on milk composition. Some studies have reported that fat content in colostrum and carbohydrate content in mature milk are significantly higher in the older mothers (≥35 yrs) as compared to the younger mothers (<35 yrs) (Hausman Kedem et al. 2013; Lubetzky et al. 2015). Similarly, carbohydrates in mature milk are reported to be positively correlated with maternal age (Lubetzky et al. 2015). In contrast, colostrum fat and energy content is shown to be negatively correlated with maternal age (Mangel et al. 2017). Colostrum fat in mothers above 35 yrs old is reported to have significantly lower saturated fatty acids and higher monounsaturated fatty acid levels as compared to younger mothers (Sinanoglou et al. 2017).

Maternal Body Mass Index

Maternal body mass index (BMI) also influences breast-feeding practice. Maternal overweight and obesity is negatively correlated with duration of breastfeeding (Driul et al. 2012). Schuster et al. suggests that milk contains a number of hormones that may influence infant metabolism. It is reported that increasing maternal BMI is associated with an increase in the concentration of leptin in breast milk suggesting risk for infant obesity in later age (Miralles et al. 2006; Andreas et al. 2014). Many studies have reported a positive correlation between breast milk leptin and adiponectin concentrations with maternal BMI and presence of these hormones in milk shows its role in infant appetite and growth regulation (Woo et al. 2009; Eilers et al. 2011; Schueler et al. 2013).

Parity

Some studies found that multiparity is significantly associated with breastfeeding and increase in milk lipid concentration (Bachour et al. 2012; Hackman et al. 2015; Kitano et al. 2016). The parity-related increase of lipid concentration is attributed to the changes in the mammary gland during successive pregnancies (Bachour et al. 2012). In contrast, milk protein concentration is reported to decrease with the increase in parity (Bachour et al. 2012). The protein composition of milk was found to be similar irrespective of mother's parity (Montagne et al. 1999). The proportion of endogenous fatty acids was shown to be lower in the milk of mothers of very high parity (Prentice et al. 1989).

Mode of Delivery

Mode of delivery includes the categories of vaginally not induced labor, vaginally induced labor, planned c-section, and unplanned c-section. It is reported that colostrum milk protein concentration is higher while fat, cholesterol and energy levels are similar in women having vaginal delivery as compared to mothers having cesarean delivery (Dizdar et al. 2014). Mode of delivery has a major impact on milk microbiome composition. It is reported that, bacterial diversity and richness are higher in milk samples from vaginal deliveries compared to c-section (Cabrera-Rubio et al. 2016). In contrast, higher total bacterial concentrations were found in colostrum and transitional milk in cesarean deliveries compared to vaginal deliveries, whereas similar concentrations were detected in mature milk samples with both modes of delivery (Khodayar-Pardo et al. 2014; Toscano et al. 2017). This shows that labor process influences milk content and galactopoiesis (Dizdar et al. 2014).

Smoking

The impact of smoking during lactation on offspring growth and development is well documented (Dahlstrom et al. 2008; Chan et al. 2016; Napierala et al. 2016). It is observed that women who smoke have lower milk production and shorter periods of lactation (Mello et al. 2001; Knudsen et al. 2001; Letson et al. 2002). Smoking during pregnancy alters milk composition by decreasing its fat and protein content (Bachour et al. 2012). Szlagatys-Sidorkiewicz et al. revealed that higher levels of milk SFA, MUFA, higher values of omega 6 fatty acids except LA and lower DHA in smoking women as compared to non-smokers (Szlagatys-Sidorkiewicz et al. 2013). IL-1β and IL-8 concentrations were reported to be lower in colostrum, while IL-6 was lower in mature milk of smoking mothers (Etem Piskin et al. 2012). Milk also contains some metals (Cd, Cr, Cu, Fe, Mn, Pb and Zn) (Nwosu et al. 2003). In the breast milk of mothers who smoke, higher concentrations of all seven trace metals were found (Kwapulinski et al. 2004).

Adverse Pregnancy Outcome

Adverse pregnancy outcome mainly include gestational diabetes mellitus, preeclampsia and pregnancy induced hypertension and preterm labor (Liu et al. 2012; Gidrewicz and Fenton, 2014; Grapov et al. 2015). These pregnancy complications are independently associated with delayed lactogenesis (Henderson et al. 2008; Chapman, 2014; Matias et al. 2014). It was also observed that women who deliver preterm and who have hypertension during pregnancy show compromised initiation of lactation due to inadequate production of hormones (Haldeman, 1993; Cregan et al. 2002).

In preterm milk, higher protein, lower lactose and similar fat concentration are reported as compared to term milk (Gabrielli et al. 2011; Gidrewicz and Fenton, 2014). Term and preterm milk have different compositions of fatty acids. Myristic, palmitic, oleic and eicosapentaenoic acid were increased in the preterm group as compared to term milk (Aydin et al. 2014). No change in magnesium while lower concentrations of calcium and phosphorus are reported in preterm and full-term milk (Butte et al. 1984). The concentrations of most cytokines and immunoglobulins are shown to be higher in the colostrum than in mature milk of women with preterm delivery (Moles et al. 2015). In the mature preterm milk samples, higher expression of neurotrophic factors was found as compared to the mature term milk samples (Collado et al. 2015).

It is reported that the composition of free amino acids in breast milk does not differ between women with gestational diabetes mellitus and healthy women (Klein et al. 2013). An observational study demonstrated that human colostrum whey proteome is different in women with and without gestational diabetes mellitus (Grapov et al. 2015). Hormones like copeptin, adropin and irisin are present in human milk and are required for homostasis. The copeptin concentration was shown to be higher while the adropin and irisin concentrations were lower in colostrum from women with GDM (Aydin et al. 2013).

It has been demonstrated that women with hypertensive diseases have significantly less breast feeding rate than control women (Leeners et al. 2005). Demirci et al. reported an association between hypertensive disorders of pregnancy and delayed onset of lactogenesis II (Demirci et al. 2018).The effect of preeclampsia on milk components is also studied. Total peroxide and oxidative stress index was shown to be higher in the milk of hypertensive pregnant women as compared to normotensive pregnant women (Erdem et al. 2012). Milk adiponectin concentration was also shown to be higher in women with preeclampsia as compared to control group (Liu et al. 2012).

Lactation Stage

Stage of lactation is one of the strong factors affecting milk composition. Changes in milk composition over the course of lactation are more significant during the first weeks of lactation. It has been shown that total energy; lactose, protein and fat contents change over the course of lactation (Yang et al. 2014). Milk protein and zinc concentrations were found to decrease whereas milk fat and folate concentrations increase as lactation progresses (Trugo et al. 1988). Similarly, there is a decline in the concentrations of many milk elements like copper, zinc, calcium and magnesium across the stages of lactation (Bates and Prentice, 1994). It has been suggested that this decline in mineral concentrations reflect lower infant needs for growth (Li et al. 2016). Most of the human milk oligosaccharide levels decrease during the course of lactation (Austin et al. 2016). The highest concentrations of carotenoids and tocopherols were found in colostrums and gradually reduce as lactation progresses (Xue et al. 2017). It has been reported that fatty acid composition of breast milk varies with lactating period, while total saturated fatty acid remain stable. However, decanoic acid and lauric acid are shown to increase over the lactation period (Jiang et al. 2016).

Behavioural Factors

Breast milk composition changes constantly even during a single feed. It also depends on the time of day and also significantly between mothers. An infant has varying degrees of appetite and thirst, because of which breast milk can vary to meet infant's nutritional requirements. It is reported that milk fat, protein and lactose concentrations are similar between left and right breast of healthy mothers (Mitoulas et al. 2002). Similarly, the fat content of milk is varying over 24 hours, whereas the level of lactose and protein content remained the same over 24 hours in the mothers of healthy term infants (Khan et al. 2013). In the comparison between foremilk and hind milk, the fat content was found to be highest in hindmilk (Saarela et al. 2005).

Infant's Gender

Interestingly, gender is also found to be associated with the milk composition. In mothers who delivered female infants, lower carbohydrate and lower calorie levels were observed within 3 months of lactation as compared to those delivering male infants (Hahn et al. 2017). In the same context, Powe et al, showed 25% greater energy content in the milk of mothers delivering male infants as compared to mothers delivering female infants (Powe et al. 2010). In contrast, other reports that milk fatty acid composition is similar in male and female infants (Sinanoglou et al. 2017).

3.7 Preeclampsia

Preeclampsia is a hypertensive disorder of pregnancy. The prevalence of preeclampsia is 8-10% of all pregnancies worldwide (Gilbert et al. 2007; Anderson et al. 2012; ACOG 2013). It is characterized by presence of hypertension and proteinuria (Ramos et al. 2017). Hypertension is defined as blood pressure above 140/90 mmHg or higher on two occasions at least 4 hours apart after 20 weeks of gestation. Proteinuria is defined as the excretion of 300mg of protein in a 24 hr urine collection or 1+ urinary protein dipstick reading (ACOG, 2013). Preeclampsia is also characterized by maternal organ dysfunction such as renal insufficiency, neurological or haematological complications, uteroplacental dysfunction, or fetal growth restriction (Mol et al. 2016). It has a high risk for maternal, fetal and neonatal morbidity and mortality (Pauli and Repke, 2015).

3.7.1 Pathophysiology of Preeclampsia

The aetiology of preeclampsia is complex and not fully understood till date. It is a multifactorial disorder of pregnancy. The primary cause of preeclampsia is thought to be inadequate placentation (Khong et al. 1986; Fisher, 2015). Placenta from women with preeclampsia have placental infarcts i.e.

interruption in blood flow between the placenta and baby and sclerotic narrowing of arterioles (Sircar et al. 2015). Defective trophoblastic invasion with uteroplacental hypoperfusion is suggested to lead to preeclampsia (Makris et al. 2007). Various studies have identified several factors in pregnant mothers that eventually lead to preeclampsia and are shown in Fig. 11.

Figure 11: Pathogenesis of Preeclampsia

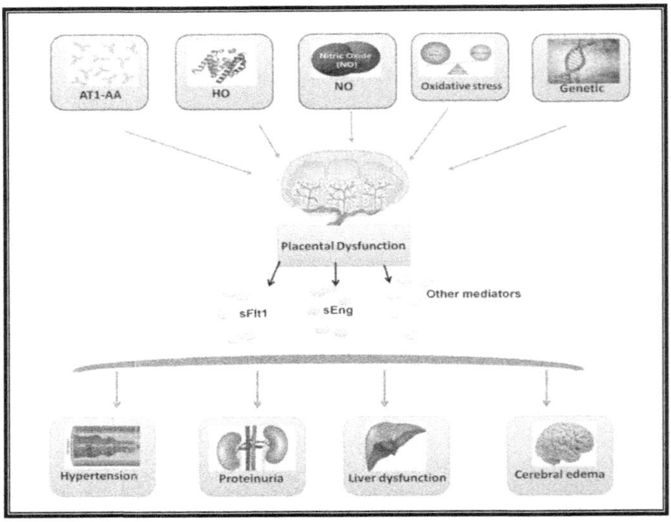

Source: *Cerdeira and Karumanchi, 2012, Cold Spring Harb Perspect Med, 2(11): a006585*

AT1-AA: agonistic autoantibodies to the angiotensin II type 1 receptor; **NO**:Nitric Oxide; **HO**:*Heme oxygenase;* **sFlt1**: Soluble fms-like tyrosine kinase-1; **nEng**: endoglin

Abnormal Trophoblast Invasion

Placenta is composed of numerous tree-like projections termed chorionic villi where maternal-fetal exchange occurs. The uteroplacental circulation is established by cytotrophoblasts (Fisher, 2015). Cytotrophoblasts invade the maternal spiral arterioles thereby remodelling the arterioles into large capacitance vessels with low resistance and thus allowing adequate placental perfusion to maintain the growing fetus (Davison et al. 2004). Impairment in the spiral artery remodeling leads to placental ischemia and increase in oxidative stress (Phipps et al. 2016). In preeclampsia, shallow or absence of remodeling of the maternal spiral arteries leads to a decrease in the blood flow thereby resulting in inadequate nutrition to the fetus (Possomato-Vieira and Khalil, 2016).

Angiogenic Factors

Normal placental development is characterized by vasculogenesis (*de novo* vascular formation during embryogenesis), angiogenesis (formation of new blood vessels from existing ones) and pseudovasculogenesis (cytotrophoblast invasion for spiral artery remodeling). During pregnancy, these physiological processes in placenta are regulated by pro and anti-angiogenic factors (Cerdeira and Karumanchi, 2012). Placenta is one of the richest sources of both proangiogenic factors like vascular endothelial growth factor (VEGF), placental growth factor (PIGF), basic fibroblast growth factor (bFGF) and transforming growth factor-β (TGF-β) and anti-angiogenic factors like Fms-Like Tyrosine Kinase 1 (sFlt1), endoglin and angiopoietins (Jardim et al. 2015). Among the angiogenic factors, VEGF plays an important role in the regulation of placental vascular development (Chen and Zheng, 2014). During normal pregnancy, human placental VEGF expression increases with gestational age (Chen and Zheng, 2014). However, in pathological conditions like in preeclampsia, lower maternal levels of VEGF and PIGF have been reported (Sahay et al. 2014). In 2003, Maynard et al., showed that, the expression of soluble fms–like tyrosine kinase 1 (sFlt-1) (a key mediator in the development of preeclampsia) and soluble endoglin (sEng) (placenta–derived protein) was higher in the placenta of women with preeclampsia than placenta derived from normal pregnancy (Maynard et al. 2003; Venkatesha et al. 2006).

Heme Oxygenase Pathway

Heme Oxygenase-1 (HO-1) and its gaseous product or metabolite i.e. carbon monoxide (CO) contributes to implantation and placentation (Zenclussen et al. 2015). HO-1 is expressed by trophoblast cells within the placental bed and its inhibition is reported to result in defective trophoblast invasion in vitro (McCaig and Lyal, 2009). HO enzyme exists in two forms, Hmox 1 and Hmox 2. Hmox levels in the placenta and exhaled CO in placental villous explants and first-trimester trophoblast cells are reported to decrease in women with preeclampsia (Ahmed et al. 2000; Baum et al. 2000).

Nitric Oxide Pathway

The vascular endothelium plays a crucial role in the maintenance of physiological vascular tone and structure. Nitric oxide (NO) is one of the major a potent vasodilator and is subsequently released from endothelial cells in response to mechanical and chemical stimuli (Johal et al. 2014). NO is formed by the activity of an enzyme NO synthase (NOS). The nitric oxide (NO)/nitric oxide synthase (NOS) system is deranged or abnormal in preeclampsia (Boger et al. 2010). Serum NO levels were shown to be lower in women with preeclampsia which may result in lower uterine artery diameter, spiral artery length and uteroplacental blood flow (Kulandavelu et al. 2012; Johal et al. 2014). Lower levels of NO (Lowe, 2000; Dai et al. 2013) and higher levels of arginase (which degrades a precursor molecule in the NOS pathway) have been reported in preeclampsia (Bernardi et al. 2008; Sankaralingam et al. 2009). Thus, it is evident that an intact NOS system is important for normal spiral artery remodelling and healthy pregnancy outcome.

Oxidative Stress

Oxidative stress is an imbalance between the formation of reactive oxygen species and antioxidants which forms the endogenous defense system (Hansson et al. 2015). In normotensive pregnant women, the source of oxidative stress is the placenta, where free radical synthesis occurs (Raijmakers et al. 2004). Free oxygen radicals are oxidative substances and they can cause structural and functional damage to cellular DNA, proteins and cell membranes (Tjoa et al. 2006; Valko et al. 2007). Lipid peroxidation, protein oxidation, DNA oxidation and higher levels of homocysteine are considered as the main causative factor for oxidative stress in preeclampsia (Serdar et al. 2003; Gohil et al. 2011; Shahbazian et al. 2016). Higher levels of oxidative stress markers have been observed in maternal circulation (Harsem et al. 2006) and in placenta (Takagi et al. 2004) of preeclamptic pregnancies.

3.8 The Developmental Origins of Health and Adult Disease (DOHaD)

The developmental origins of adult health and disease hypothesis states that environmental factors, act in early life (conception, pregnancy, infancy and childhood) to programme the risks for adverse health outcomes (McMillen et al. 2008) as depicted in Fig. 12.

Figure 12: Concept of Developmental Origins of Health and Diseases and Risk for Diseases

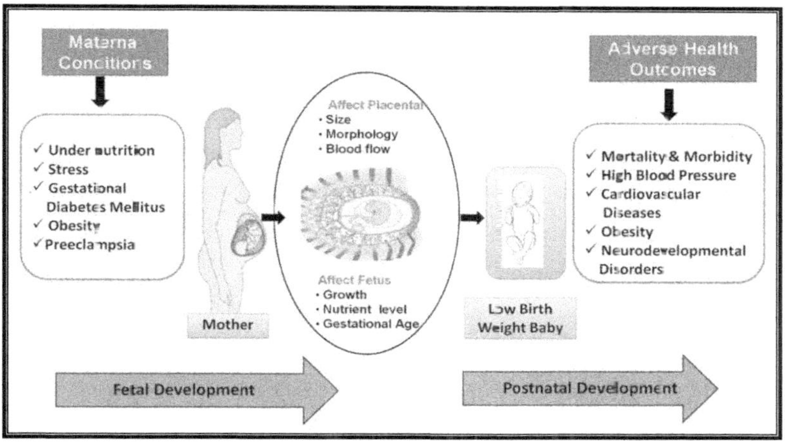

Source. *Chavatte-Palmer et al. 2016, Int. J. Environ. Res. Public Health, 13(6):586*

Prenatal exposure to preeclampsia is shown to be associated with an increased risk of hypertension in young adults (Davis et al. 2012; Herrera-Garcia and Contag, 2014). The risk of obesity also seems to be higher in offspring with prenatal exposure to preeclampsia (Davis et al. 2012). Increasing evidence suggests that neurodevelopment can be altered by fetal environment (Krakowiak et al. 2012; Maher et al. 2017). An association between gestational environmental factors such as preeclampsia and some neurodevelopmental impairments and metabolic diseases, has been observed in earlier studies (Krakowiak et al. 2012; Ryckman et al. 2013).

3.8.1 Consequences of Preeclampsia on Mother and their Children

Preeclampsia is associated with various maternal consequences which include both acute and long-term effects. Acute maternal complications are stroke, abruptio placentae or disseminated intravascular coagulation, haemolysis, elevated liver enzymes, low platelet count syndrome (HELLP), pulmonary edema, adult respiratory distress syndrome and acute renal failure death (Amaral et al. 2015). Long-term maternal complications are chronic hypertension, diabetes mellitus, chronic renal failure, coronary artery disease, neurologic deficit and premature death (Neiger, 2017). There is a high prevalence of cardiovascular and cardiopulmonary complications in later life of women affected by preeclampsia (Bauer and Gerss, 2009; Riise et al. 2017).

Preeclampsia is known to affect the health of the offspring both in early and later life (Bokslag et al. 2016). In preeclampsia, placental hypoperfusion (decreased blood flow through an organ) can cause fetal growth restriction and oligohydramnios (deficiency of amniotic fluid) (Bokslag et al. 2016). Babies born to mothers with preeclampsia often have low birth weight (Szymonowicz and Yu, 1987; Odegard et al. 2000; Sutherland et al. 2014). A higher fetal death rate was observed in women with preeclampsia versus uncomplicated pregnancies (Bokslag et al. 2016). The risk of stillbirth is sevenfold higher in pregnancies with preeclampsia compared to normotensive pregnancies (Harmon et al. 2015). Preeclampsia is also considered as a significant contributor to preterm birth (birth before 37 weeks of gestation) (Davies et al. 2016). Preterm birth is the world's leading cause of neonatal morbidity and mortality and low birth weight (LBW) infants (Goldenberg et al. 2008). The risk of preterm birth in women with preeclampsia is four times higher than women without preeclampsia (Davies et al. 2016). Prematurity and a small body size at birth are associated with mental disorders (Abel et al. 2010) like schizophrenia and mood disorder. Furthermore, LBW infants delivered to mothers with preeclampsia are reported to have lower cognitive and executive functioning in childhood, adolescence and adulthood (Silveira et al. 2007) (Fig. 13).

Figure 13: Short Term and Long Term Consequences of Preeclampsia

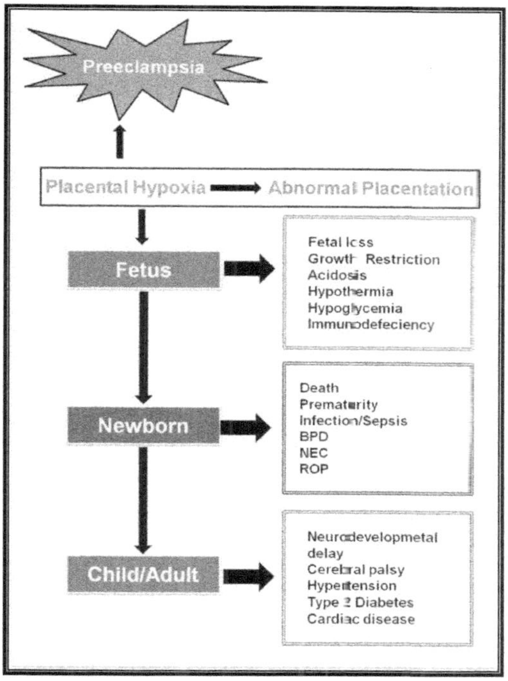

Source: *Lin et al. 2015, Transl Res, 165(4):449-463*

BPD: Bronchopulmonary dysplasia; **NEC**: Necrotizingenterocolitis
ROP: Rretinopathy of prematurity

Short term neonatal effects of preeclampsia include an increased risk of hematological abnormalities, such as thrombocytopenia and polycythemia (Bhat and Cherian, 2008). Long term effects are associated with higher rates of infant respiratory distress syndrome, intraventricular haemorrhage, sepsis, bronchopulmonary, necrotizing enterocolitis dysplasia, retinopathy of prematurity and neurodevelopmental disability in childhood (Saigal et al. 2008; Cetinkaya et al. 2012; Shulman et al. 2017).

3.8.2 Preeclampsia and Risk for Neurodevelopment Disorders of Children

Reports suggest that hypertensive disorders of pregnancy (gestational hypertension and preeclampsia) are associated with neurocognitive outcomes in middle childhood especially verbal ability and behavioral problems (Robinson et al. 2009; Whitehouse et al. 2012). It has also been reported that infants born to women with preeclampsia have a lower median mental developmental index (MDI) compared with the control group (Schlapbach et al. 2010). Walker et al. showed a strong association between fetal exposure to preeclampsia and development of autism spectrum disorder and developmental delay in children (Walker et al. 2015). Similarly, a longitudinal cohort study demonstrated that infants born to mothers with severe preeclampsia have neurodevelopmental delays up to 3 yrs of age (Warshafsky and Pudwell, 2016). In contrast, it is reported that mild preeclampsia is not associated with adverse neurodevelopmental disorders in offspring (Warshafsky and Pudwell, 2016). In 2009, data from the Danish Medical Birth Registry showed that prenatal exposure to gestational hypertensive disorders was associated with slightly reduced adult cognitive performance (Ehrenstein et al. 2009). Silveira et al. showed that neurodevelopmental outcome was better in infants born to preeclamptic mothers than controls at 18 months corrected age (Silveira et al. 2007). In contrast, preeclampsia was associated, with a lower risk of any mental disorder in the male offspring (Tuovinen et al. 2012). It is also reported that maternal hypertensive disorders of pregnancy does not increase the risk of long-term neurodevelopmental complications in infants at 2-3 yrs of age (Matic et al. 2017). It is also reported that there is no significant difference between any of the neurocognitive parameters (IQ, school achievements, and neurodevelopmental score) in children at 9-10 yrs between the preeclampsia, maternal hypertension and normotensive IUGR groups. (Leitner et al. 2012).

3.9 Brain Development

The brain is the most complex organ due its intricate structure and function. Brain acts as a control center by receiving, interpreting, and directing sensory information throughout the body. Neural development begins shortly after conception and continues throughout the life span (Stiles and Jernigan, 2010).

During this period, major neurodevelopmental events occur and it includes neuronal cell proliferation, differentiation, migration and synaptic connections, which are important for the development of cognitive functions (Chen et al. 2015). Fig.14 summarizes the landmark events during prenatal (conception to birth) and postnatal (birth to adulthood) neural development.

Figure 14: Timeline of Major Events in Brain Development

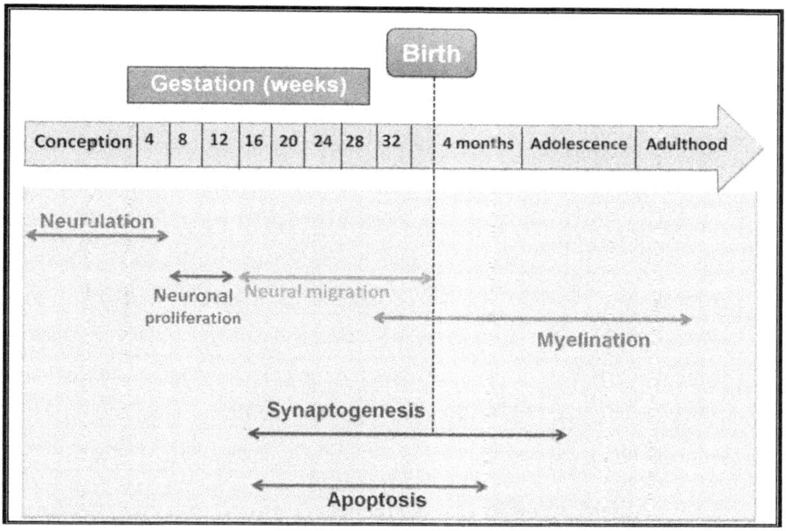

Source: *Tau and Peterson, 2010, Neuropsychopharmacology, 35(1):147–168*

3.9.1 Embryonic and Fetal Brain Development

The first key event in the development of the central nervous system is the formation of the neural tube which connects the brain and spinal cord (Couperus and Nelson, 2006). The neural tube formation completes by 3 to 4 weeks of gestation and from 4 to 12 weeks it starts differentiating into various components of the nervous system. Cell division begins within the neural tube and production of nerve cells (neurons) and glial cells (cells that support neurons) also takes place. As neurons are produced, they migrate to different brain areas where they begin to make connections with other neurons establishing neural networks. The neurons communicate with each other via connections called synapses (Kolb and

Gibb, 2011). Any disturbances in these processes can alter neuronal structure and function which can lead to neurodevelopmental disorders and that affect a child's behaviour, memory or ability to learn.

3.9.2 Postnatal Brain Development

Brain development continues for an extended period postnatally. Infants are born with their neurons which are already formed and the differentiation and maturation of these cells continues throughout childhood (Stiles and Jernigan, 2010). In the early postnatal yrs, synapses are also overproduced (Tau and Peterson, 2010). Most of the communications that take place between a brain neuron that transmits a signal and one that receives that signal occur at synapses (Wurtman, 2014). The process of myelination starts at 29th week of gestation and continues up to 2 yrs. The brain reaches 80% of its adult size during this period (Knickmeyer et al. 2008). The brain increases in size by four-fold during the preschool period, which appears to be related to the rapid development of motor skills that occurs during this period (Stiles and Jernigan, 2010). Postnatal brain maturation involves dynamic changes in both gray and white matter (Giedd et al. 1999; Sowell et al. 2004). There is high demand of biochemical precursors and nutrients for the process of rapid neural growth (Wang, 2009; Wang, 2012).

3.9.3 Nutrition and Brain Functioning

Adequate nutrition is necessary for normal brain development. Nutrition is especially important during pregnancy and infancy which are crucial periods for the formation of the brain (Prado and Dewey, 2014). Nutrients are known to affect a number of processes in the brain by regulating neurotransmitter and hormone metabolism pathways, synaptic transmission and signal-transduction pathways. (Bhatnagar and Taneja, 2001; Lozoff and Georgieff, 2006; Gómez-Pinilla, 2008). All nutrients are important for neuronal cell growth and development, but some appear to have greater effects during the late fetal and neonatal periods. These include protein, iron, zinc, selenium, iodine, folate, vitamin A, choline, and LCPUFA. Most importantly, all these are found in the breast milk and also play a key role in the brain development of the infant (Fig.

15). Extensive literature suggests a link between breastfeeding and positive neurodevelopmental gains.

Figure 15: Breast Milk Components and Brain Development of Children

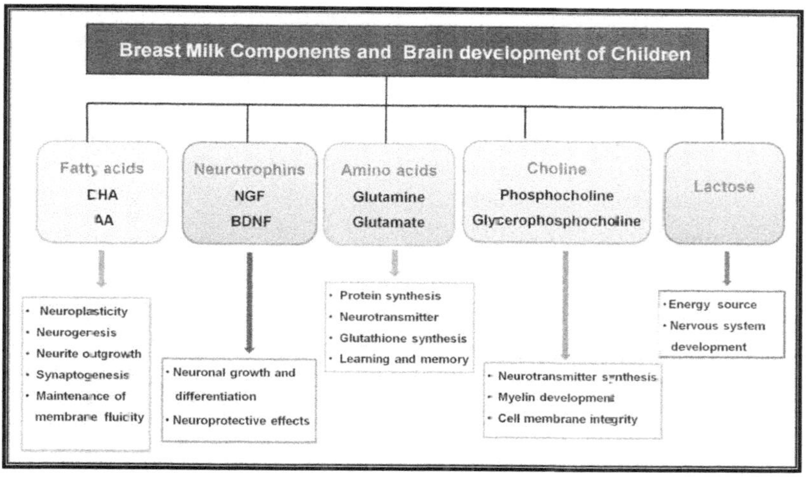

3.10 Breastfeeding and Neurodevelopment in Children

The relationship between breastfeeding and neurodevelopmental outcome was first discussed in 1929 when Hoefer and Hardy examined the mental and physical outcomes of children aged 7 to 13 yrs. They concluded that children who had been breastfed for 4 to 9 months outperformed in intelligence, educational achievement, motor and language development (Hoefer and Hardy, 1929). Since then, the association between breastfeeding and increased cognitive development for children has been widely acknowledged. Specifically, Horwood and Fergusson observed a positive relationship between breastfeeding and a variety of beneficial educational outcomes (Horwood and Fergusson, 1998). It has been reported that children who were mostly breastfed for more than 6 months had higher test scores at 10 yrs of age as compared to non-breastfed children (Oddy et al. 2010). In a group of Asian toddlers, increased exposure to breastfeeding was associated with higher scores on tests of both expressive and receptive language (Cai et al. 2015) and higher scores in cognitive, language and motor development at 18 months of age among Greek toddlers (Leventakou et al. 2013).

Observational studies have reported positive association of breastfeeding with later intelligence (Jain et al. 2002; Ip et al. 2007; Kanazawa, 2015; Horta et al. 2015).

The duration of breastfeeding is also shown to be associated with cognition. Longer duration of breastfeeding, particularly full breastfeeding is reported to have beneficial effects on child neuropsychological (Michaelsen et al. 2009) and with higher verbal and nonverbal IQ at 7 yrs of age (Belfort et al. 2013). Increasing duration of breastfeeding showed gradual increase in cognitive developmental score from infancy through the preschool age (Jedrychowski et al. 2012). In school-aged children (8-11 yrs) who were breast fed, a positive association was found between learning skills like speaking, reading, writing, spelling and mathematical calculation as compared to the never-breastfed children (Kim et al. 2017).

Breastfeeding in the first 2 months of life is shown to be associated with structural markers of brain development in infants. Smaller ventricular volume and larger head circumference were also found for exclusively breastfed babies (Herba et al. 2013). Breastfed children exhibited increased white matter development, neural growth and parietal cortex from 10 months through 4 yrs of age (Deoni et al. 2013; Kafouri et al. 2013). Recent reports reveal improved myelination in breastfed children accompanied by increased general, verbal, and non-verbal cognitive abilities compared to children who were exclusively formula-fed (Deoni et al. 2018). Deoni et al. provided MRI evidence that breastfed infants exhibit better development in specific brain areas associated with language and visual reception abilities compared to those who are fed formula or a mixture of breast milk and formula (Deoni et al. 2013). In contrast, a comprehensive review by the Agency for Healthcare Research and Quality summarized 400 articles (out of 9000 abstracts) and found that breastfeeding has few or small effects on children's cognitive performance (Ip et al. 2007).

3.10.1 Breast Milk Fatty Acids and Brain Development in Children

LCPUFA are involved in neurogenesis, neuronal migration, gliogenesis, synaptogenesis, and myelination from the stage of fertilization. Both DHA and AA account for approximately 20% of brain fatty acid content and are involved in early neurodevelopment by promoting neural development, repair and myelination. In infancy, breast milk provides sufficient amounts of LCPUFA to meet the child's requirements (Koletzko et al. 2008). Analysis of milk samples from 28 countries showed that breast milk DHA makes a highly significant contribution to cognitive performance (Lassek and Gaulin, 2015).

Several studies have reported that high DHA concentrations in breast milk is associated with a better ability to adjust to changes in surrounding, better mental development, improved hand-eye coordination, better attention scores and memory performance in children (Helland et al. 2003; Jensen et al. 2005; Hart et al. 2006; Dalmeijer et al. 2016). Children with a longer duration of breastfeeding had significantly higher mental scores than children with low breastfeeding duration (Guxens et al. 2011). Studies have shown that, high levels of LA in colostrum are associated with poor motor and cognitive scores (2-3 yrs) and negatively associated with Verbal IQ (5-6 yrs) (Bernard et al. 2015; Bernard et al. 2017). However, child attention scores were better at five yrs of age in the group of children whose mothers had received LCPUFA supplementation (Campoy et al. 2012; Delgado-Noguera et al. 2015).

3.10.2 Breast Milk Neurotrophins and Brain Development in Children

Reports indicate that neurotrophins like NGF and BDNF are present in breast milk (Li et al. 2011; Collado et al. 2015; Velasco et al. 2016; Wani et al. 2017). It is reported that milk BDNF levels were higher in colostrum than mature milk (Collado et al. 2015). The source of BDNF in milk is not clear and there is a need for further research to understand the role of leukocyte-derived BDNF production. It mediates neuronal plasticity, migration, and survival in both the central and peripheral nervous system (Bramham and Messaoudi, 2005; Greenberg et al. 2009). It has been shown that the presence of neurotrophic factors (BDNF and GDNF) in human milk is not affected by the consumption of multivitamins (Velasco et al. 2016). In spite of their crucial role in the developing central nervous system (Bartkowska et al. 2010) there are no studies on role of breast milk neurotrophins and cognitive assessment in children.

3.10.3 Milk Metabolites and Brain Development in Children

Glutamate is an important neurotransmitter that plays a key role in long-term potentiation, synaptic plasticity and is important for cognitive functions like learning and memory (Sapolsky, 2005). An adequate amount of glutamate is critical for the glutathione syntheses which act as an antioxidant. The role of glutathione is also crucial for the development of the fetus. It has been reported that altered glutathione levels make infants more vulnerable to developmental damage (Choe et al. 2001).

Choline is a critical micronutrient that plays a pivotal role in neurotransmitter synthesis, myelin development, and cell membrane integrity (Zeisel, 2004). Choline is a precursor of the endogenous neurotransmitter acetylcholine and disturbances of the acetylcholine system may impair hippocampus-related cognitive and emotional function (Busche et al. 2006). The possible role of milk choline status on neurodevelopment in children has been investigated. Higher milk choline with higher DHA was related to better recognition memory in infants (Cheatham and Sheppard, 2015).

Carbohydrate composition (lactose–isomaltulose) is known to influence some aspect of cognitive performance such as attention and memory (Taib et al. 2012). However, till date there are no studies on milk lactose levels in women with preeclampsia.

3.11 Cognition

The word cognition is derived from the Latin word "cognito," which means "to think." Cognition is "the mental action or process of acquiring knowledge and understanding through thought, experience, and the senses. Learning and memory are fundamental cognitive skills and are thought to be continuous processes. In a definition proposed by Dr. Eric Kandel, "Learning is the process by which we acquire knowledge. Memory is the process by which knowledge is encoded, stored and retrieved. Cognition is a basic neurological process and can be defined as the set of processes that enable us to gain information about our environment- processes such as learning, memory, reasoning and problem solving. Memory is a complex network of various interconnected functions like classification, encoding, storage and retrieval of wide variety of information (Paul et al. 2009).

3.12 Cognitive Tests

Modern cognitive tests originated through the work of James McKeen Cattell who coined the term "mental tests". Cognitive tests are used to determine a child's learning capability by identifying their cognitive strengths and weaknesses. Cognitive development is assessed by a variety of standard cognitive tests based on various age groups because the developmental abilities vary as per their age group (Kaufman and Kaufman, 2004). Several frequently used tests used and are briefly described in Table 1.

Table 1: Tests of Cognition

INSTRUMENT	Type	Age
Bayley Mental Development Index	Development	1-42 months
McCarthy Scales of Children's Abilities General Cognitive Index	Intelligence	2.6-8.6 yrs
Stanford Binet Intelligence Scale	Intelligence	2 yrs – adult
Peabody Picture Vocabulary Test	Intelligence, Educational	2.5 yrs - adult
Wechsler Preschool and Primary Scale of Intelligence	IQ-Multitask	3-7 yrs
Kaufman Assessment Battery for Children	Intelligence and Academic Skills	3-18 yrs

Kaufman Assessment Battery for Children

The Kaufman Assessment Battery for Children - Second Edition (KABC-II; Kaufman and Kaufman, 2004) is widely accepted and used. The test was developed by Alan S. Kaufman and Nadeen L. Kaufman in 1983 and revised in 2004. It tests cognitive processing abilities of children and adolescents. The

KABC-II is a theory-based clinical instrument and has been used in different cultural settings. The KABC-II, developed in 2004, was based on the data-driven Catell-Horn-Carroll (CHC) and clinically-driven Luria theoretical models. The CHC model is a research-based psychometric theory that categorizes special cognitive abilities. The CHC model provides a global score called the Fluid-Crystallized Index (FCI) and the Mental Processing Index (MPI). The Luria global ability score is called the MPI (Kaufman and Kaufman, 2004). The KABC-II consists of five domains of intelligence, which are represented in the form of scale indexes: Simultaneous, Sequential, Learning, Planning, and Knowledge Scales (Fig.16). The five areas include

Figure 16: Structure of KBAC II

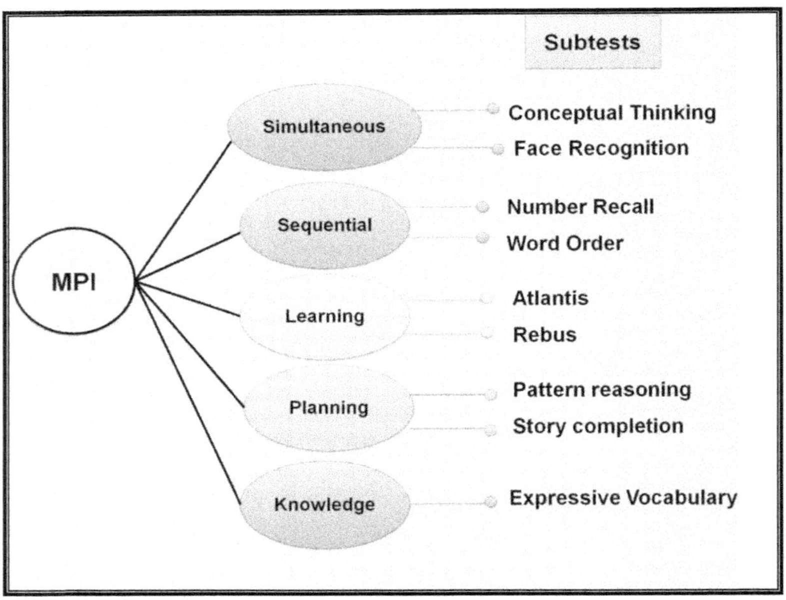

MPI: Mental processing index

(1) Simultaneous processing

Simultaneous processing is the mental process which is used to integrate separate bits of information. Processing a person's face, maps and graphs, having a good sense of direction, and being able to see how puzzle pieces fit together are examples of simultaneous processing (e.g. face recognition) (Fig. 17).

Figure 17: Face Recognition

(2) Sequential Processing

Sequential processing is a term used to describe the processing that occurs in the order that it is received. (e.g. word order, number recall) (Fig. 18).

Figure 18: Word Order

- Book - - - Cup
- Cup - - - House - - - Bird
- Book - - - Bird - - - House - - - Cup

(3) Learning

Learning is the process of acquiring new or modifying existing knowledge, behaviors, skills, values, or preferences. (e.g. Atlantis) (Fig. 19).

Figure 19: Atlantis

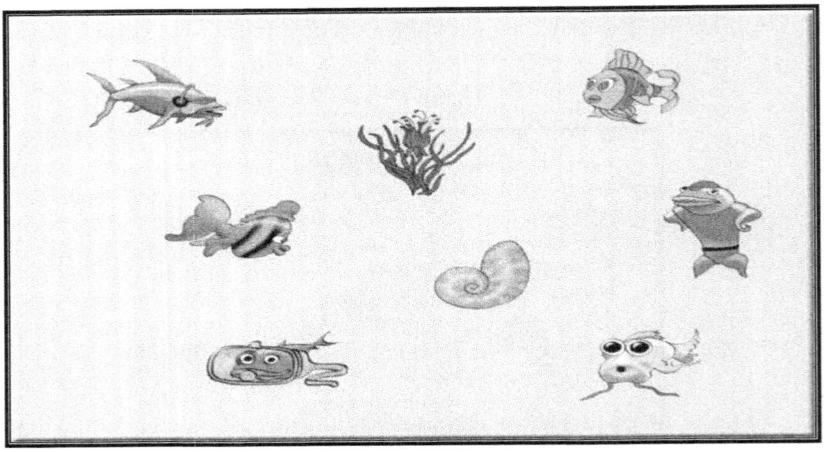

(4) Planning

In this, the child is shown a series of stimulus that form a logical linear pattern with one stimulus missing. The child has to select the missing stimulus from several options (e.g. Pattern Reasoning) (Fig. 20).

Figure 20: Pattern Reasoning

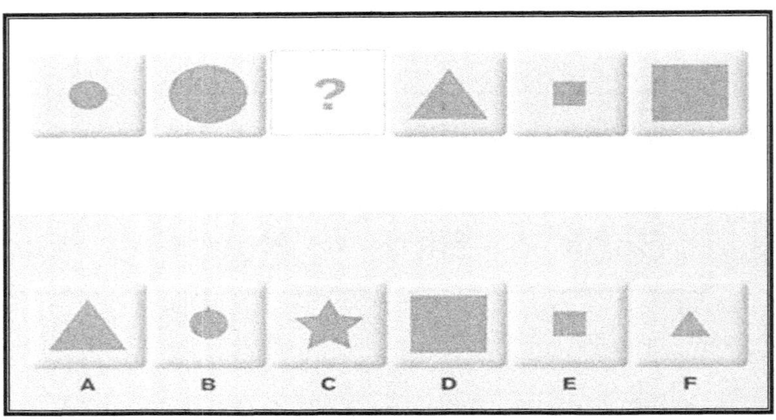

(5) Knowledge

Knowledge is a familiarity, awareness, or understanding of someone or something, such as facts, information, descriptions, or skills (e.g. Riddles, verbal knowledge, and expressive vocabulary tests) (Fig. 21).

Figure 21: Expressive Vocabulary

This clinical instrument consists of 16 subtests where 10 are mental processing subtests and 6 achievement subtests. Not all subtests are administered to each age group. Hunt (2005) concluded that the majority of KABC-II subtests are good for measures of knowledge, long-term and short-term memory, and visual processing (Hunt et al. 2005).

Children born to mothers with preeclampsia are suggested to be at risk for developing cognitive and behavioral disorders in later life. Studies till date suggest that the constituents of human milk play vital role in early brain development which may have significant implications in later life. Neural maturation of breast fed infants is known to be linked to breast milk LCPUFA concentrations. In spite of this, it is unclear whether milk LCPUFA, neurotrophins and other metabolites are altered across lactation in pregnancy complications like preeclampsia. Therefore, the present study for the first time examines the levels of these breast milk components at various time points across lactation in mothers with preeclampsia. The association of these breast milk components with growth and cognitive performance in the children is also assessed.

The next chapter describes the materials and methods used in the present work.

CHAPTER 4
MATERIALS AND METHODS

This chapter describes the detailed study design and methodology used for the biochemical estimations from breast milk. It also describes the tests used for assessing cognition in children.

4.1 Ethics Approval and Enrolment

This study was approved by Bharati Vidyapeeth Medical College Institutional Ethics Committee (BVU/Exam/5608/2009-10 and BVDU/MC/86A-2/9/2014). This prospective study was carried out at Interactive Research School for Health Affairs (IRSHA), Bharati Vidyapeeth (Deemed to be University). Singleton pregnant women with preeclampsia (n=101) and normotensive women (control) (n=144) were recruited at the time of delivery at the Departments of Obstetrics and Gynaecology. A written informed consent was taken from each subject. Patients were recruited with the following inclusion and exclusion criteria.

4.1.1 Inclusion Criteria

Women in the age group 18-35 yrs with singleton pregnancies and women with preeclampsia were also included in this study. The control group consisted of pregnant women with no medical or obstetrical complications.

4.1.2 Exclusion Criteria

Women with any pregnancy complication, history of non-communicable diseases like diabetes mellitus, renal diseases, hypertension, cardiovascular disease, seizure disorder, renal or liver disease, bleeding disorders and HIV, HBsAg positive were excluded from the study. Alcohol or drug abuse in the pregnant women was also considered as an exclusion criterion.

4.1.3 Definition and Diagnosis of Preeclampsia

Preeclampsia was defined by systolic and diastolic blood pressures greater than 140 and 90 mm/Hg, respectively, with proteinuria (> 1+ or 300 mg/24 hr) in a dipstick test. Edema was present in some cases. Blood pressure was measured in the left arm with a mercury sphygmomanometer. Preeclampsia was confirmed by repeated recording of the blood pressure with an interval of six hours.

The gestational age in the current study was determined by last menstrual period and ultrasound measurement. Cases with a discrepancy of more than a week between clinical and ultrasound readings were excluded from the study. Both preeclamptic and normotensive women were from a lower socioeconomic group.

4.2 Dietary Assessments

Food Frequency Questionnaire (FFQ) was administered at all time points in all lactating women to assess the frequency of consumption of foods. All lactating women had to indicate the frequency of each food consumed during the last one month for which scores were calculated. The questionnaire consisted of 17 food groups and a number of food items (approximately 10) were listed under each of the food groups. The frequency of intake of foods was recorded on an eight point scale from "never" to "thrice daily". Monthly scores were calculated for each food item. For example, an item consumed once a week had a score of 4 while that consumed daily had a score of 30. These foods were identified using "Nutritive Values of Indian Foods" (Gopalan et al. 1996; Gopalan, 2003). The food frequency questionnaire has been used by our department in a number of studies on pregnant women (Kilari et al. 2009; Kilari et al. 2010; Kulkarni et al. 2011).

4.3 Collection and Storage of Samples

Maternal venous blood (10 ml) was collected into the ethylenediamine tetra acetic acid (EDTA) vials just before delivery. All blood samples were immediately layered on histopaque (a density gradient obtained from Sigma-Alderich) and centrifuged at 2000 rpm for 30 minutes to separate the plasma and erythrocytes. The plasma and erythrocyte aliquots were stored at -80°C until further analysis.

Milk sampling was done at all time points during lactation (day 3, 1.5 mo, 2.5 mo, 3.5 mo and 6 mo). Samples of breast milk (2 ml) were taken from mother and stored at −80°C.

4.3.1 Follow up of Infants

The infants were followed-up at day 3, 1.5 mo, 2.5 mo, 3.5 mo and 6 mo of age at Departments of Paediatrics, Bharati Hospital, Pune. The anthropometry (weight, length, head and chest circumference) of the infant was recorded at all time points by standard techniques. Fig. 22 shows the number of milk samples analyzed for fatty acids, neurotrophins and other metabolites at various time points during lactation.

Figure 22: Flow Chart Showing the Number of Milk Samples Analyzed for Fatty Acids, Neurotrophins and Other Metabolites at Various Time Points During Lactation

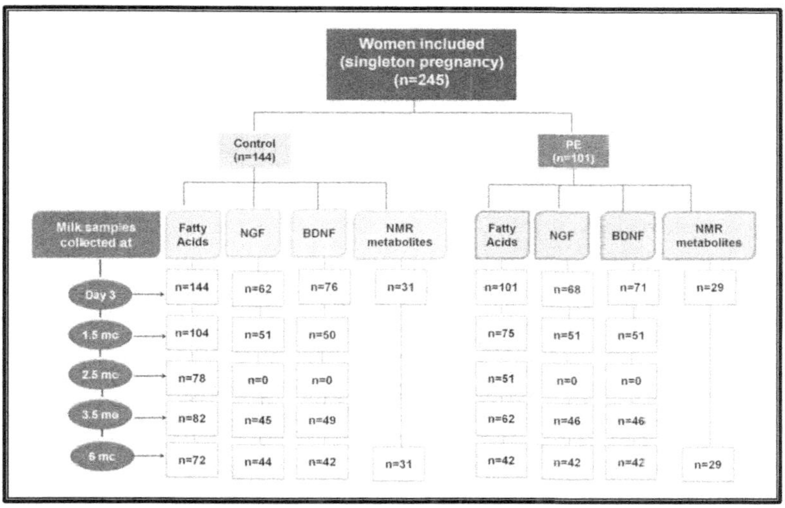

PE: Preeclampsia

4.4 Biochemical Estimations

4.4.1 Plasma and Milk Fatty acids

Plasma and milk fatty acid methyl esters were prepared and fatty acids were analyzed by the modified method of Manku et al. (Manku et al. 1983).The method is also described in detail in our earlier departmental studies (Dangat et al. 2010; Mehendale et al. 2008). Briefly, transesterification of the milk samples was carried out using hydrochloric acid-methanol. These were separated and quantified using Perkin Elmer gas Chromatograph (SP 2330, 30-m capillary Supelco column, Perkin Elmer, Shelton, CT, USA). Helium was used as a carrier gas at 1 ml/min. Oven temperature was held at 150^0C for 10 min, programmed to rise from 150^0 to 220^0 C (at 10^0 C/min), and then held at 220^0 C for 10 min. The detector temperature was 275^0 C and the injector temperature was 240^0 C. Peaks were identified by comparison with standard fatty acid methyl esters (Sigma-Aldrich). Fatty acids were reported in g/100 g. A total of 15 fatty acids were estimated. Saturated fatty acids included myristic acid, palmitic acid and stearic acid while monounsaturated fatty acids included myristoleic, palmitoleic, oleic and nervonic acids. The omega 3 fatty acids included alpha-linolenic acid (ALA), eicosapentaenoic acid (EPA) and docosahexaenoic acid (DHA) while omega 6 fatty acids included linoleic acid (LA), gamma-linolenic acid (GLA), dihomo-gamma-linolenic acid (DGLA), docosapentaenoic acid (DPA) and arachidonic acid (AA).

4.4.2 Plasma and Milk Nerve Growth Factor (NGF)

Plasma and milk NGF levels were measured using the Emax Immuno Assay System Promega kit (Zettler et al. 1996). The method has been reported by us earlier (Kilari et al. 2011). Briefly, the NGF Emax® Immunoassay system is designed for the sensitive and specific detection of NGF in the antibody sandwich format. In this format, the plates were coated with anti-NGF polyclonal Antibody (pAb) and kept overnight for incubation at 4^0C. Next day, after washing once, block and sample buffer was added to block non-specific binding. The standards and test samples were then added and plates were incubated with shaking at room temperature for 6 hrs to allow binding of soluble NGF to the immobilized anti-NGF pAb. The plates were washed 5 times, after which anti-NGF monoclonal antibody (mAb) was added to bind captured NGF and incubated overnight at 4^0C. Next day, after washing 5 times, a species-specific antibody (anti-rat IgG) conjugated to horseradish peroxidase (HRP) is added to detect the amount of specifically bound mAb. The plates were incubated with shaking for 2.5 hrs at room temperature. After washing, the chromogenic substrate was then added to measure the colour change followed by the stop solution. The colour developed was read at 450 nm using an ELISA plate reader (BioRad). NGF concentrations were expressed as pg/ml.

4.4.3 Plasma and Milk Brain Derived Neurotrophic Growth Factor (BDNF)

Plasma and milk BDNF levels were measured using the BDNF Emax Immuno Assay System Promega kit (Hornbeck, 1994). The method has been reported by us earlier (Pillai et al. 2010; Dhobale et al. 2012). This assay employs sandwich ELISA method, in which 96 well plates were coated with anti-BDNF mAb and kept overnight at 4^0C. After washing once, block and sample buffer was added to block non-specific binding followed by the addition of standards and test samples. The plates were incubated with shaking at room temperature for 2 hrs. The plates were then washed 5 times, after which BDNF pAb was added and incubated at RT for 2 hrs. Anti-IgY antibody conjugated to HRP was used as a tertiary reactant to enable detection of bound pAb. For this, again the plates were incubated (with shaking) for 1 hour at RT. The plates were washed 5 times to remove unbound conjugate. The chromogenic substrate was added to detect the colour change. The reaction was stopped using 1N hydrochloric acid. The amount of BDNF was directly proportional to the colour observed and was read at 450 nm using an ELISA plate reader. BDNF concentrations were expressed as pg/ml.

4.4.4 Milk Metabolites

Nuclear Magnetic Resonance spectroscopy (NMR)

Proton NMR was used to identify 25 milk metabolites (alpha-lactose, beta-lactose, oligosaccharides, myo-inositol, alanine, glutamate, glutamine, glycine, histidine, isoleucine, leucine, lysine, phenylalanine, tyrosine, valine, acetone, citrate, creatine, phosphocreatine, acetate, choline, lactate, lipid, phosphocholine and glycerophosphocholine). For NMR spectroscopy, the milk samples were thawed and shaken thoroughly to homogenize the sample. 50 μL of milk was mixed with 520 μL of D2O and formate (0.5mM) was added to the sample that served as a concentration reference. Sodium trimethyl-silyl-[2, 2, 3, 3-H4] propionate (TSP) (0.5 mM) was added to the sample, that served as a chemical shift reference for the proton NMR studies. It has been reported that TSP interacts with the proteins (such as albumin) present in biological samples (Ando et al. 2010). Alpha-lactalbumin (albumin present in milk) is the major protein in breast milk, which may bind with TSP and thus may influence the accurate quantitative determination of metabolites (Pearce et al. 2008). Therefore, in this study, formate was used as concentration reference while TSP was used only as the chemical shift reference.

The ^{1}H NMR experiments of milk samples were performed on 700 MHz spectrometer (Agilent Technologies, Santa Clara, U.S.A.). One-dimensional (1D) 1H spectrum with water suppression were acquired with a single 90^0 pulse. The typical parameters for 1D experiment were: spectral width of 9124.1 Hz, data points 32K, number of scans 16. Since, the longitudinal relaxation time (T1) value of formate is 12.7 s at 700 MHz, a relaxation delay of 70 s was used to attain complete relaxation for appropriate quantification of metabolites. The data was processed on a Dell 390N, PC, Red Hat Enterprise Linux workstation using the Varian software, Vnmrj 3.2A (Agilent Technologies, Santa Clara, U.S.A.). The free induction decays were multiplied by an exponentially decaying function prior to Fourier transformation. The value of LB is 0.3 Hz. Spectra were manually phased using zero and first order corrections. Water resonance was suppressed using the pre-saturation pulse at the water frequency.

Two-dimensional (2D) double quantum filtered correlation spectroscopy (DQF COSY) and total correlation spectroscopy (TOCSY) experiments were also carried out at 700 MHz for few samples for unambiguous assignment of various resonances. This helps in identifying the complete networks of spin couplings in a molecule. TOCSY experiment was carried out using the following parameters: 2K data points in F2 dimensions, spectral width of 9124.1 Hz, relaxation delay of 2 s and mixing time of 80ms, 200 times domain points (number of experiments) were collected in t1with 16 acquisitions. The parameters for 2D DQF COSY experiments were 2K data points in F2 dimensions, spectral width of 9124.1 Hz, relaxation delay of 2 s and 200 time domain points (number of experiments) were collected in t1 with 16 acquisitions.

Quantification of the Metabolites

The concentration of the metabolites was determined by comparing the integrated intensity of isolated resonance of the compounds of interest with that of the formate signal. In this study, we could not determine concentration using Chenomx software as it uses, 2, 2-dimethyl-2-silapentane-5-sulfonate (DSS) or 3-(trimethylsilyl) propionic acid (TSP) for the quantification of metabolites. A total of 14 metabolites (alpha-lactose, beta-lactose, alanine, glutamate, glutamine, glycine, acetate, choline, phosphocholine, glycerophosphocholine, acetone, citrate, creatine,and phosphocreatine) were quantified from NMR spectra of human milk samples. These metabolites were classified as sugars (alpha-lactose and beta-lactose), amino acids (alanine, glutamine, glutamate and glycine), fatty acids and their metabolites (acetate, choline,phosphocholine, glycerophosphocholine) and energy metabolites (acetone, citrate, creatine and phosphocreatine).

4.5 Anthropometric Measurement of Infants

Infant weight was recorded using a digital weighing scale (Zeal Medical Private Limited, India) and baby length was measured to the nearest 0.1 cm using a portable infantometer. Head circumference was determined by placing a fiber glass measuring tape around the head, just above the eyebrows (or eyebrow ridges) anteriorly and around the most prominent bulge posteriorly. Chest circumference was measured by placing the measuring tape on the lower chest of the baby.

4.6 Cognitive Assessment of Children

Cognition was assessed using The Kaufman Assessment Battery for Children (KABC II) at 3-6 yrs of age (Kaufman and Kaufman, 2004; second edition). This battery of tests is validated for Indian children (Veena et al. 2010). KABC II is a theory based clinical instrument. This covers domains (area) of learning, long-and short-term memory and retrieval, reasoning, language, visuo-spatial ability, visuo-motor processing, attention and concentration. All these tests were administered by a trained master level psychologist in the local language, in a single session of 60–90 minutes in the morning in a quiet room. It is composed of 18 subtests that lead to separate scoring based on each of the models. In the current study we included the following subtests shown in Table 2.

Table 2: Subtests of Kaufman Assessment Battery

Name of the Test	Description	Cognitive Abilities
Word order	The child points to a series of silhouettes of common objects in the same order as mentioned by the examiner	Short term memory, Memory span, working Memory
Atlantis	The child is taught nonsense names for fish, plants and shells, and is asked to point to the named object among an array of pictures	Long-term memory Learning ability/ and retrieval, associative memory
Conceptual thinking	The child selects one picture from a set of 4 or 5 which does not belong with the set.	Measures classification ability in an nonverbal format
Face recognition	The child looks a photographs of one or two faces for 5 seconds and then selects the correct face/faces shown in a difference pose from a selection.	Visual processing
Expressive Vocabulary	Measures the Childs ability to say the correct names of objects and illustrations.	Expressive knowledge of Child

4.7 Power of the Study

The power of the current study was calculated based on our previous study which examined levels of milk DHA ($p<0.05$) between normotensive women ($n=82$) and women with preeclampsia ($n=41$) (Dangat et al. 2010). The sample size in the current study gives a power of 88% with 0.05 type I error probability.

4.8 Inter and Intra Assay Variability

The intra- and inter-assay variability of all biochemical parameters was less than 10% coefficients of variance.

4.9 Statistical Analysis

The data was analyzed using SPSS/PC+ package for MS Windows (Version 20, Chicago, IL). Levels of various milk components and developmental scores were expressed as mean ± standard deviation (SD). The 'Shapiro–Wilk' test was used to test the variables for normality distribution. Skewed variables were transformed to satisfy the underlying assumption of normality using natural logarithm transformation (log e). Mean values of the estimates of milk metabolites between the groups (control and preeclampsia) at different time points across lactation were compared by Student's -t test. The degree of significance is denoted by the value of p, and is considered statistically different when $p\leq 0.05$.

Correlations between milk fatty acids and neurotrophins with baby weight, length, head and chest circumference were studied using Pearson's correlation analysis after adjusting for maternal age, body mass index (BMI) and duration of gestation. Associations of milk fatty acids and neurotrophins with cognition of children were also studied using Pearson's correlation analysis.

CHAPTER 5
RESULTS

This chapter reports the levels of various breast milk components in mothers with preeclampsia and compares them with normotensive control women. Further, the associations of these milk components with growth parameters and cognitive performance in children are also reported.

5.1 Maternal and Neonatal Characteristics

Table 3 shows the maternal and neonatal characteristics. The systolic and diastolic blood pressure was higher ($p<0.01$ for both) in the preeclampsia group as compared to the normotensive control group. Baby weight, length, head and chest circumference at birth were lower in preeclampsia group as compared to control ($p<0.01$ for all).

Table 3: Maternal and Neonatal Characteristics

Maternal Characteristics	NC (n=144)	PE (n=101)
Age (yr)	24.0 ± 3.7	23.7 ± 3.6
Income (INR)	7784 ± 4720	7593 ± 5086
BMI (kg/m^2)	24.6 ± 4.12	25.7 ± 5.16
Gestation (wk)	39.2 ± 1.04	36.9 ± 2.83 **
Sys BP (mmHg)	120.11 ± 9.17	151.18 ± 18.48 **
Dia BP (mmHg)	77.64 ± 6.1	99.27 ± 10.4 **
Parity [n (%)]		
Nulliparous	57(39.6)	68(65.4)
Multiparous	85(59.0)	33(31.7)
Mode of Delivery [n (%)]		
Vaginal	109(76.8)	41(41.8)
C-section	33(23.2)	57(58.2)
Maternal education (%)		
Illiterate	5.6	5.8
Primary	7.6	4.8
Secondary	47.2	51.0
Higher secondary	18.8	21.2
Graduate	20.1	16.3
Post graduate	0.7	1.0
Neonatal Characteristics at Birth		
Weight (kg)	2.89 ± 0.29	2.26 ± 0.73**
Length (cm)	48.17 ± 2.49	45.13 ± 3.60**
HC (cm)	33.54 ± 1.31	31.7 ± 2.55**
CC (cm)	32.12 ± 1.46	28.89 ± 3.67**

NC: Normotensive control; **PE**: Preeclampsia; **BMI**: Body mass index; **Sys BP**: Systolic blood pressure; **Dia BP**: Diastolic blood pressure; **HC**: Head circumference; **CC**: Chest circumference

Values given are mean ± SD. **$p<0.01$ when compared to normotensive control

5.2 Frequency of Consumption of ALA, DHA and Omega-3 Fatty Acid Rich Foods

In our cohort, the alpha-linolenic acid (ALA) rich foods consumed by the women include pulses (e.g., cowpea, rajma) and green leafy vegetables (e.g., fenugreek, spinach, colocasia leaves, amaranth, ambat chukka) while fish consumption was considered as a docosahexaenoic acid (DHA) rich food. The frequency of consumption of ALA rich foods was similar in both the normotensive control and preeclampsia groups at all time points i.e. at delivery, 1.5 mo, 2.5 mo, 3.5 mo and 6 mo of lactation. Similarly, the frequency of consumption of DHA and omega 3 rich foods was also similar at all time points of lactation.

5.3 Maternal Plasma LCPUFA Levels

The levels of ALA ($p<0.05$), DHA ($p<0.01$) and total omega 3 fatty acids ($p<0.01$) were lower in the preeclampsia group as compared to control group. However, there was no change in the levels of omega 6 fatty acids, saturated fatty acids (SFA) and monounsaturated fatty acid (MUFA) levels and has been reported by us earlier (Roy et al. 2014).

5.4 Maternal Plasma Neurotrophin Levels (BDNF and NGF)

Maternal plasma brain derived neurotrophic factor (BDNF) levels were significantly lower ($p<0.01$) in women with preeclampsia as compared to control. Similarly, lower ($p<0.01$) plasma nerve growth factor (NGF) levels were observed in the preeclampsia group as compared to control (Fig. 23).

Figure 23: Maternal Plasma Neurotrophins Levels

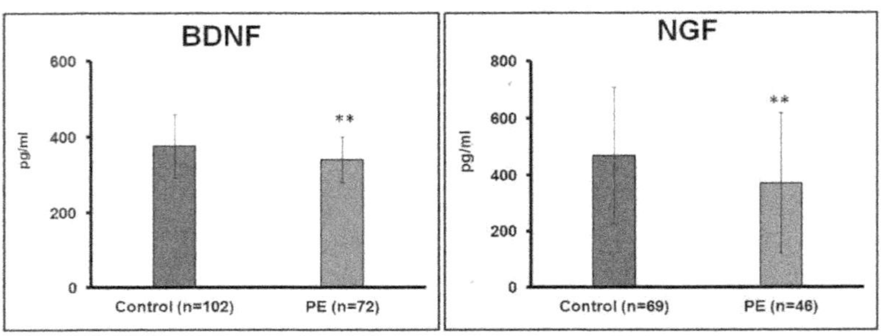

Values are Mean ± SD; p: significance $^{**}p<0.01$ when compared to control

5.5 Milk Fatty Acid Levels in Control and Preeclampsia Groups at Various Time Points of Lactation

Milk linoleic acid (LA) (a precursor of arachidonic acid (AA)) levels were lower but not statistically significant at all time points except at 2.5 mo in women with preeclampsia as compared to control (Fig. 24). However, milk AA levels were similar in the preeclampsia group as compared to control at all time points. The levels of ALA (a precursor of DHA) were similar in the preeclampsia group as compared to the control group. In contrast, milk DHA levels were higher ($p<0.05$ for all) at day 3, 1.5 mo and 3.5 mo in women with preeclampsia as compared to control (Fig. 24). The levels of omega 3 fatty acids, MUFA and SFA did not differ between the groups while total omega 6 fatty acid levels were lower at 2.5 mo ($p<0.05$) in preeclampsia group.

Milk fatty acid levels (LA, AA, ALA, DHA, SFA, MUFA, Omega 3 and Omega 6 fatty acids) at 6 mo of lactation were similar between the groups (Fig. 24)

Figure 24: Milk Fatty Acids Levels at Various Time Points of Lactation

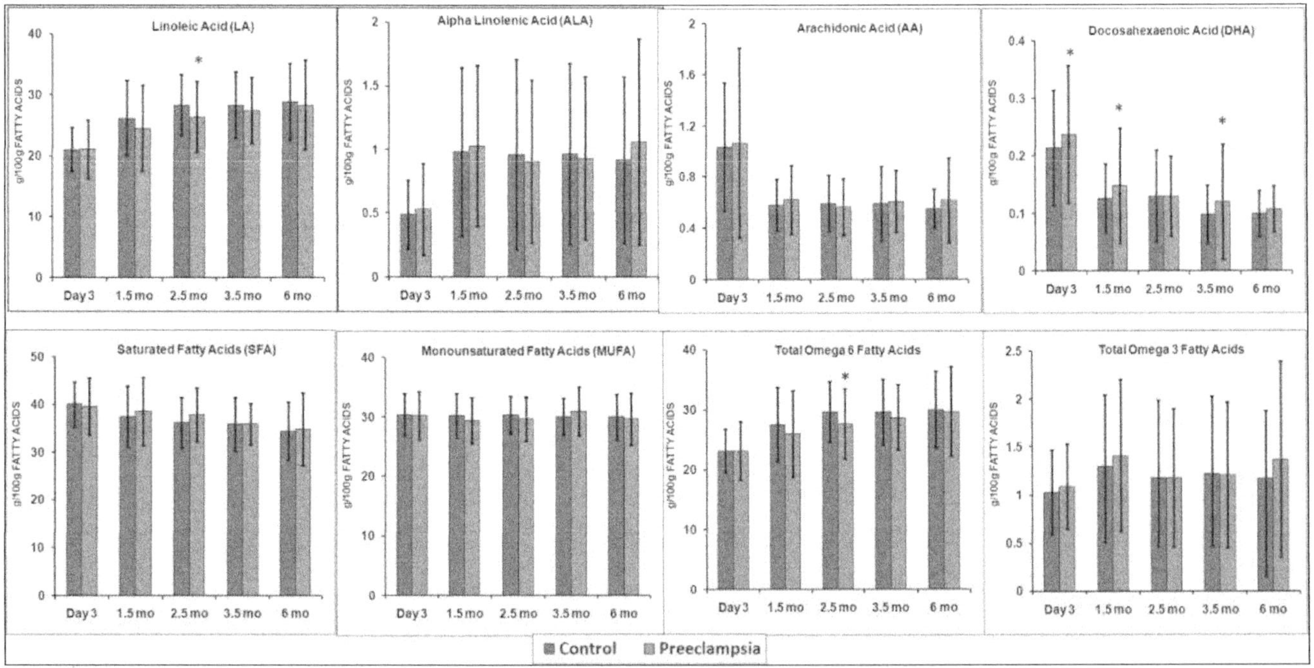

Values are Mean ± SD; p: significance *p<0.05 when compared to control

5.6 Milk Fatty Acid Levels in Women Consuming Vegetarian and Non-Vegetarian Diets

In the present study, 29.2% women consumed a vegetarian diet while 70.8% women consumed a non-vegetarian diet in the normotensive control group. In the preeclampsia group, 33.7% women consumed a vegetarian diet while 66.3% women consumed a non-vegetarian diet.

At day 3 of lactation, the levels of milk AA ($p<0.05$), DHA ($p<0.01$) and omega 3 ($p<0.05$) fatty acids were higher in the normotensive control women consuming a non-vegetarian diet as compared to women consuming a vegetarian diet (Fig. 25). However, there was no change in milk AA, DHA, and omega 3 fatty acids in women with preeclampsia consuming a non-vegetarian diet as compared to women consuming a vegetarian diet. Further, there was no difference in the levels of above fatty acids between normotensive control and preeclampsia women consuming vegetarian and non-vegetarian diets.

Figure 25: Milk Fatty Acid Levels at Day 3 in Women Consuming Vegetarian and Non-vegetarian Diets

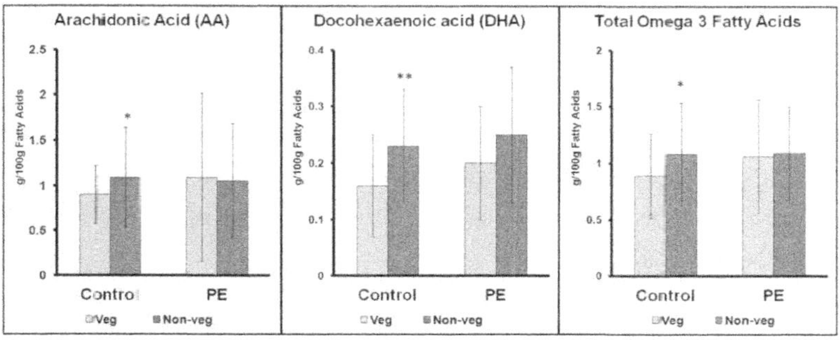

PE: Preeclampsia; **Veg**: Vegetarian; **Non-veg**: Non-vegetarian

Values are Mean ± SD; p: significance. $^{**}p<0.01$ and $^{*}p<0.05$ when compared to normotensive control consuming vegetarian diet

At 6 mo of lactation, all fatty acids were similar in normotensive control women consuming vegetarian and non-vegetarian diets (Fig. 26). However, omega 3 fatty acids were higher ($p<0.05$) in the group of women with preeclampsia consuming vegetarian diet compared to normotensive women consuming vegetarian diet. The levels of other fatty acids i.e. SFA, MUFA and omega 6 were similar in women with preeclampsia and normotensive control women consuming vegetarian and non-vegetarian diets at both day 3 and 6 mo of lactation.

Figure 26: Milk Fatty Acid Levels at 6 month in Women Consuming Vegetarian and Non-vegetarian Diets

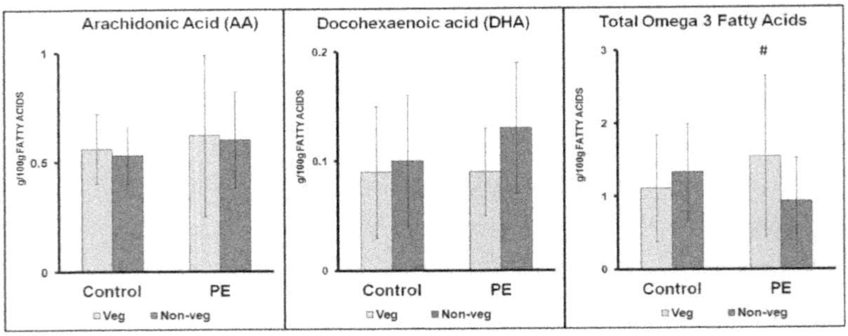

PE: Preeclampsia; **Veg:** Vegetarian; **Non-veg**: Non-vegetarian

Values are Mean ± SD; p: significance. $^{\#}p<0.05$ when compared to normotensive control consuming vegetarian diet

5.7 Milk Neurotrophin Levels in Control and Preeclampsia Groups at Various Time Points of Lactation

At day 3 of lactation, milk BDNF levels were significantly higher ($p<0.05$) in the preeclampsia group as compared to control group. In contrast, there was no change in milk NGF levels in the preeclampsia group as compared to the control group.

The levels of both NGF and BDNF in control and preeclampsia also show different longitudinal patterns. Milk NGF levels were significantly lower at 1.5 and 3.5 mo in preeclampsia group as compared to control. However, milk NGF levels remain lower but not significant between the groups at 6 mo. In contrast, milk BDNF levels were significantly lower at 1.5 mo in preeclampsia as compared to control. However, there was no significant difference in milk BDNF levels between groups at 6 mo of lactation (Fig. 27).

Figure 27: Milk Neurotrophin Levels at Various Time Points of Lactation

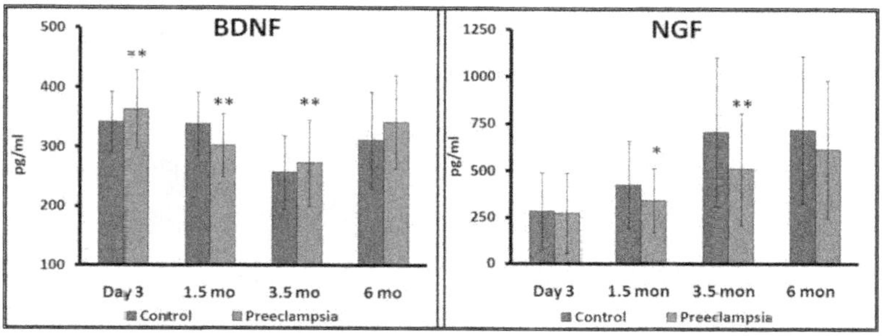

BDNF: Brain derived neurotrophic factor; **NGF:** Nerve growth factor

Values are Mean ± SD; p: significance. $^{*}p < 0.05$; $^{**}p < 0.01$ when compared to normotensive control

5.8 Milk Neurotrophins Levels in Women Consuming Vegetarian and Non- Vegetarian Diets

The levels of milk NTs (NGF and BDNF) were similar between women consuming vegetarian and non-vegetarian diets in both the groups (normotensive control and preeclampsia).

5.9 Metabolic Profile of Milk

Fig. 28 shows the representative 1D ^{1}H NMR spectra of milk of women with preeclampsia. Assignments of the resonances from various metabolites like alpha-lactose, beta-lactose, myo-inositol, oligosaccharides, alanine, glutamate,glutamine, glycine, histidine, isoleucine, leucine, lysine, phenylalanine,tyrosine, valine, acetate, choline, phosphocholine, glycerophosphocholine, lactate, lipid, acetone, citrate, creatine and phosphocreatine were carried out using 1D and 2D COSY and TOCSY (spectrum not shown) and by comparing the chemical shift values reported in the literature (Sundekilde et al. 2013; Praticò et al. 2014). Both COSY and TOCSY were used for peak assignment. A COSY spectrum provides the information about the coupled nuclei which are 2–3 bonds apart in a molecule. In a TOCSY experiment, additional information is obtained as cross peaks are seen not only for nuclei which are directly coupled, but also between nuclei which are connected by a chain of couplings or till 6–7 bonds apart in a molecule. This helps in identifying the complete networks of spin couplings in a molecule. We have also identified peaks which corresponded to resonances from HMOs namely from 3′fucosyllactose (3′FL) lacto-N-fucopentaose V (LNFPV), lacto-N-difucohexose I (LNDFHI) and branched and lacto-N-fucopentaose I (LNFPI) and branched (Praticò et al. 2013). These peaks appear at: 5.39 ppm arising from H1′ of fucose (α1–3) αGlc and 5.45 ppm from H1′ of fucose (α1–3) βGlc from 3′FL, LNFPV. The peak at 5.19 ppm correspond to from H1′ of fucose (α1–2) αGalactose of LNDFHI and branched while the peak at 5.32 ppm correspond to from H1′ of fucose (α1–2) αGlc of LNFPI and branched (Praticò et al. 2014).

Figure 28: 1D ^{1}H NMR Spectrum of Milk of Women with Preeclampsia

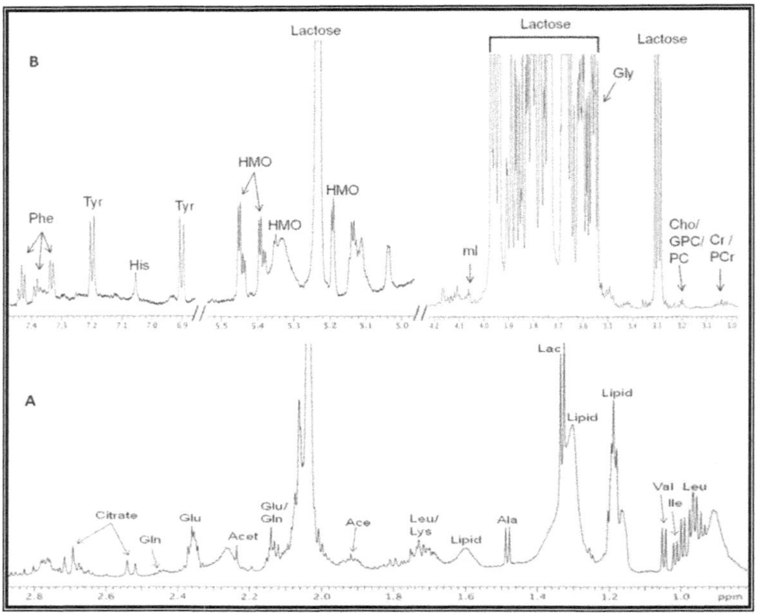

Figure. (A) shows the expanded region (0.5–2.8 ppm) of one-dimensional ^{1}H NMR spectrum of milk of patients with preeclampsia (day 3), (B) shows the expanded regions from 3.0 to 4.2 ppm, 5.0–5.5 ppm and 6.9–7.5 ppm, acquired at 700 MHz in D2O.

Leu: leucine; **Ile:** isoleucine; **Val:** valine; **Lac:** lactate; **Ala:** alanine; **Lys:** lysine; **Ace:** Acetate; **Glu:** glutamate; **Gln,** glutamine; **Acet:** acetone; **Cr:** creatine; **PCr:** phosphocreatine; **Cho:** choline; **GPC:** lycerophosphocholine; **PC:** phosphocholine; **Gly:** glycine; **mI:** myo-inositol; **HMO:** human milk oligosaccharide; **Tyr:** tyrosine; **His:** histidine; **Phe:** phenylalanine

5.9.1 Multivariate Analysis

Multivariate analysis was carried out using 200 points (bins) between the ranges of the selected milk spectral region 0.5–5.5 ppm as discussed earlier. The initial PCA using bin data showed a trend in separation between preeclampsia patients and controls in the scores plot of first two principal components (Figs. 29 A, E, 30 A and E). In the next step, a supervised PLS-DA model was built using preeclampsia /controls as a response variable (Fig. 30).

Score plot of the first two components (factor 1 and 2) of PLS-DA model demonstrated separate clusters of the samples obtained at day 3 and at 6 mo of lactation from controls (Fig. 29B) (R2=0.98,Q2=0.96) exhibiting a change in metabolic profile of milk as lactation progresses. The corresponding loading plot suggested that the separation was due to changes in lactose, glycerophosphocholine, glutamate, glutamine, oligosaccharides and creatine in multivariate analysis (Fig. 29C and D). Similarly, milk samples from preeclampsia patients obtained at day 3 and 6 mo exhibited distinct clusters along the PC1 direction on PLS-DA score plot (R2=0.96, Q2=0.90) (Fig. 29F). The variation in oligosaccharides, lactose, acetate, creatine and citrate contributed for separation (Fig. 29G and H).

The PLS-DA model also demonstrated a grouping of samples from preeclampsia and control group at day 3 (R2=0.94, Q2=0.61) (Fig. 30B) and as well as at 6 mo (R2 =0.93, Q2= 0.61) (Fig. 30F). The differences in the relative levels of oligosaccharides, lactose, acetate and acetone were the main metabolites for the separation between the two groups at day 3 (Fig. 30C and D). The changes in the levels of oligosaccharides, lactose, glutamate, glutamine and glycerophosphocholine have contributed for the discrimination of preeclampsia and control group at 6 mo (Fig. 30G and H).

Figure 29: Multivariate Analysis Plots Showing Clusters of Milk Samples from Control and Preeclampsia Groups at Day 3 and 6 mo of Lactation

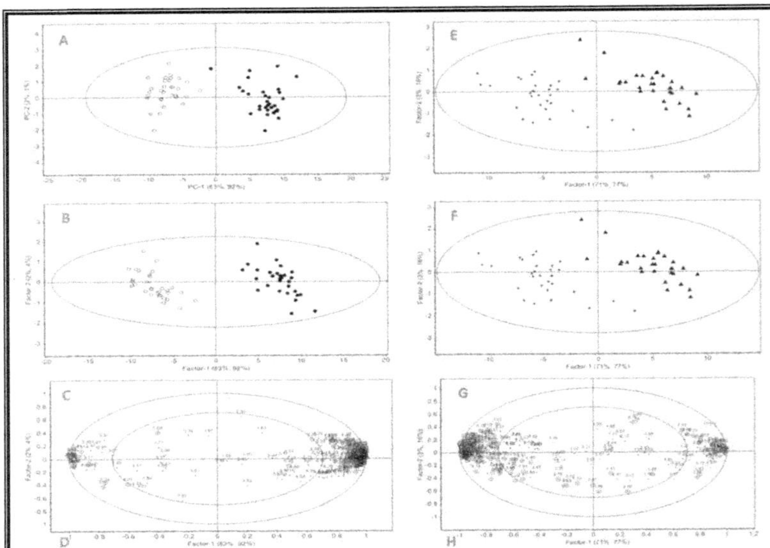

D

Metabolites	Discriminant Bins (ppm)
HMO	1.13, 1.21, 2.05,2.07,2.09, 4.27, 4.31, 4.35, 5.31, 5.33, 5.35, 5.45
Glutamate/Glutamine	2.11, 2.13
Glutamine	2.47
Glycerophophocholine	3.25
Lactose	3.67, 3.69, 3.79, 3.81, 3.89
Creatine	3.95

H

Metabolites	Discriminant Bins (ppm)
HMO	1.15, 1.19, 2.01, 2.03, 4.31, 4.33, 5.01, 5.03, 5.05, 5.09, 5.11, 5.39,5.41
Acetate	1.95
Citrate	2.59, 2.73
Lactose	3.15, 3.27, 3.41, 3.43, 3.49, 3.53, 3.65, 3.67, 3.79, 3.81

A, B, C and D represent PCA score plot, PLS-DA score plot, PLS-DA loading plot and table of discriminant metabolites and bins, respectively, at day 3 (•) and6mo (o) in control group. E, F, G and H show PCA score plot, PLS-DA score plot, PLS-DA loading plot and table of discriminant metabolites and bins, respectively, at day 3 (*) and 6 mo (▲) in preeclampsia group.

Figure 30: Multivariate Analysis Plots Showing Clusters of Milk Samples from Preeclampsia and Control Groups

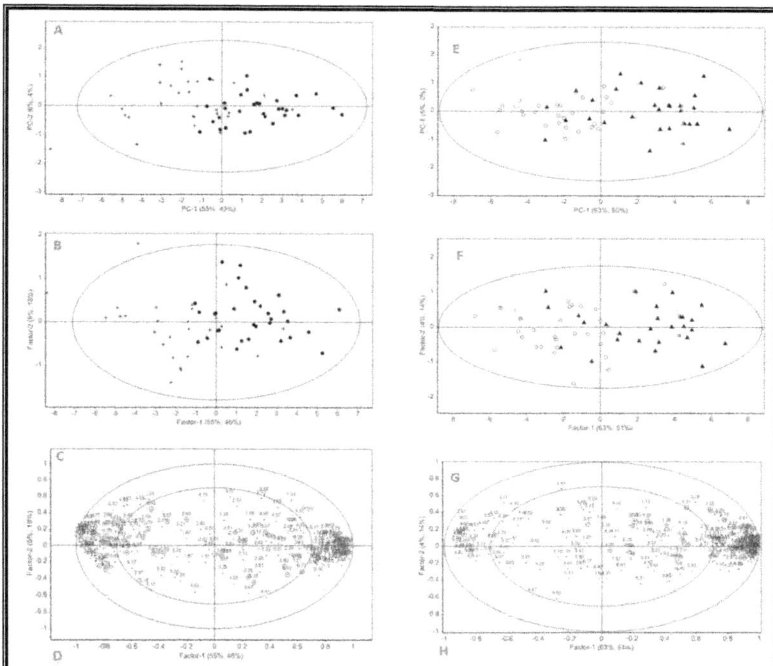

D

Metabolites	Discriminant Bins (ppm)
HMO	1.15, 1.17, 2.05, 5.05, 5.11, 5.31, 5.35, 5.39
Glutamate/Glutamine	2.13
Acetone	2.23
Lactose	3.25, 3.55, 3.73, 3.87, 4.55

H

Metabolites	Discriminant Bins (ppm)
HMO	1.19, 4.27, 5.19
Glutamate/Glutamine	2.19
Glycerophosphocholine	3.25
Lactose	3.79, 3.83, 3.87

A, B, C and D represent PCA score plot, PLS-DA score plot, PLS-DA loading plot and table of discriminant metabolites and bins, respectively, for preeclampsia (*) and control group (•) at day 3 of lactation E, F, G and H show PCA score plot, PLS-DA score plot, PLS-DA loading plot and table of discriminant metabolites and bins, for preeclampsia (▲) and control group (o) at 6 mo.

5.10 Levels of Milk Metabolites

The concentration of various metabolites observed in the milk of controls and women with preeclampsia at birth and at 6 mo are given in Table 4. To gain further insight into absolute change of levels of metabolites among groups, we have also compared the concentration of metabolites that also contributed for separation of groups in multivariate data analysis as shown in loading plots (Figs. 29 & 30). However, the concentration of metabolites could be determined only for unique peaks which did not show any spectral overlap. The levels of sugars in milk (alpha-lactose and beta-lactose) increased ($p<0.01$ for both) at 6 mo as compared to day 3 of lactation in the control group. The levels of amino acids in milk such as glutamate ($p<0.05$), glutamine ($p<0.05$) and glycine ($p<0.01$) increased at 6 mo of lactation as compared to day 3 of lactation in the control group. The level of acetate decreased ($p<0.05$); while the levels of phosphocholine ($p<0.05$) and glycerophosphocholine ($p<0.01$) levels increased at 6 mo as compared to day 3 of lactation in the control group. The energy metabolites of milk like acetone ($p<0.05$) and creatine ($p<0.01$) levels decreased (Table 4) at 6 mo of lactation as compared to day 3 of lactation in the control group. The levels of sugars (alpha-lactose and beta-lactose) and amino acids did not change at 6 mo as compared to day 3 of lactation in the preeclampsia group. The levels of fatty acid metabolites such as acetate decreased ($p<0.01$) while glycerophosphocholine levels increased ($p<0.01$) at 6 mo of lactation as compared to day 3 of lactation. Energy metabolites like creatine ($p<0.05$) and citrate ($p<0.01$) decreased at 6 mo as compared to day 3 of lactation in the preeclampsia group (Table 4).

The milk metabolites levels were similar between preeclampsia and control groups on day 3 of lactation even after adjusting for gestation. At 6 mo of lactation, the sugar levels in milk (alpha-lactose and beta-lactose) decreased ($p<0.01$ for both) in the preeclampsia group as compared to controls. Amino acids like glycine decreased ($p<0.01$) in the preeclampsia group as compared to control at 6 mo of lactation. Fatty acid metabolites such as glycerophosphocholine decreased ($p<0.01$) in the preeclampsia group as compared to controls at 6 mo of lactation. In contrast, at 6 mo of lactation, the energy metabolites like milk creatine ($p<0.05$) increased in the preeclampsia group as compared to control group (Table 4).

Table 4: The Concentration of Metabolites in Milk (mM/L) from Controls and Women with Preeclampsia at Day 3 and at 6 mo of Lactation

Milk Metabolites	At Day 3		At 6 mo	
	Control (n=31)	Preeclampsia (n=29)	Control (n=31)	Preeclampsia (n=29)
Sugars				
Alpha-lactose	47.96 ± 25.45	53.27 ± 19.07	74.38 ± 9.02$^{\#\#}$	60.41 ± 16.97**
Beta-lactose	22.12 ± 11.79	34.98 ± 37.31	38.38 ± 8.16$^{\#\#}$	30.50 ± 9.46**
Amino acids				
Alanine	1.52 ± 1.07	1.40 ± 0.57	1.26 ± 0.63	1.32 ± 0.56
Glutamate	2.98 ± 1.87	3.50 ± 1.38	3.26 ± 0.75$^{\#}$	2.95 ± 0.98
Glutamine	1.07 ± 0.58	1.24 ± 0.73	1.41 ± 0.59$^{\#}$	1.39 ± 0.56
Glycine	9.26 ± 4.82	10.72 ± 3.93	14.27 ± 2.04$^{\#\#}$	11.59 ± 3.49**
Fatty acids and associated metabolites				
Acetate	0.47 ± 0.34	0.55 ± 0.26	0.32 ± 0.13$^{\#}$	0.33 ± 0.19$^{@@}$
Choline	0.28 ± 0.23	0.29 ± 0.26	0.25 ± 0.13	0.26 ± 0.16
Phosphocholine	0.36 ± 0.32	0.44 ± 0.39	0.43 ± 0.21$^{\#}$	0.39 ± 0.18
Glycero-phosphocholine	0.17 ± 0.18	0.22 ± 0.16	0.59 ± 0.22$^{\#\#}$	0.44 ± 0.21$^{**@@}$
Energy Metabolites				
Acetone	0.85 ± 0.72	0.77 ± 0.44	0.57 ± 0.25$^{\#}$	0.61 ± 0.27
Citrate	2.52 ± 1.49	3.14 ± 1.63	2.13 ± 0.66	2.09 ± 0.85$^{@@}$
Creatine	0.24 ± 0.17	0.26 ± 0.15	0.14 ± 0.09$^{\#\#}$	0.18 ± 0.09$^{*@}$
Phosphocreatine	0.19 ± 0.11	0.19 ± 0.15	0.15 ± 0.10	0.18 ± 0.09

PE: Preeclampsia

Values are Mean ± SD; p: significance. $^{*}p<0.05$; $^{**}p<0.01$ when compared to normotensive control; $^{\#}p<0.05$; $^{\#\#}p<0.01$ (Day 3 Vs 6 mo in control); $^{@}p<0.05$; $^{@@}p<0.01$ (Day 3 Vs 6 mo in Preeclampsia)

Milk HMO levels did not change at 6 mo as compared to day 3 of lactation in both controls as well as in preeclampsia groups. The milk HMO levels were not significantly different in women with preeclampsia (0.78 ± 0.75) as compared to control group (0.86 ± 0.70) at 6 mo of lactation. The levels of milk HMO in women with preeclampsia (1.36 ± 1.27) is similar to normotensive women (1.13 ± 1.34) even after adjusting for gestation at day 3 of lactation. These HMO levels were adjusted for gestation using linear regression model and found that there is no significant difference between groups at day 3 of lactation.

5.11 Levels of Milk Metabolites in Women Consuming Vegetarian and Non-vegetarian Diets

At day 3 of lactation, the levels of milk metabolites were comparable between the normotensive women consuming vegetarian and non-vegetarian diets. However, women with preeclampsia consuming a non-vegetarian diet showed higher acetone and acetate levels as compared to women consuming a vegetarian diet.

5.12 Associations of Milk Fatty Acids with Baby Characteristics during Lactation

There was no association of milk fatty acids with baby characteristics at day 3 of lactation. However, milk AA levels were negatively associated with baby weight ($r = -0.284$, $p = 0.017$, $n=68$) at 1.5 mo and 3.5 mo ($r=-0.396$, $p=0.003$, $n=52$) in the preeclampsia group. In the control group there was positive association between milk AA and baby length ($r = 0.231$, $p = 0.045$, $n=74$) at 3.5 mo. However, such association was not seen in preeclampsia group. Milk DHA levels were negatively associated with baby length ($r=-0.363$, $p=0.007$, $n=52$) at 3.5 mo in the preeclampsia group. Saturated fatty acid levels were negatively associated with baby weight at 3.5 mo ($r=-0.268$, $p=0.050$, $n=52$) in preeclampsia group. However, these associations were not seen at 6 mo of lactation.

5.13 Associations of Milk Neurotrophins with Baby Characteristics during Lactation

There was a negative association between milk NGF and baby length at 1.5 mo only in the control group ($r=-0.337$, $p=0.019$, $n=48$). There was no association between milk BDNF and baby characteristics.

5.14 Associations of Milk Neurotrophins with Milk Fatty Acids

There was a negative association between milk NGF and milk DHA levels ($r = -0.311$, $p=0.033$, $n=47$) in the control group while milk NGF was negatively associated with milk AA ($r=-0.463$, $p=0.008$, $n=32$) in preeclampsia group at 1.5 mo of lactation. Similarly, milk NGF levels were negatively associated with milk omega 6 fatty acids ($r=-0.543$, $p=0.001$, $n=32$) in control group at 3.5 mo. However, milk BDNF levels did not show any association with milk fatty acids.

5.15 Anthropometric Measurement in Children from Birth to 3-6 yr of Age

The weight of infant was lower in the preeclampsia group at day 3, 1.5 mo and at 2.5 mo of lactation ($p<0.01$ for all) as compared to control group. However, weight was similar at 3.5, 6 month of lactation and has been reported by us (Roy et al. 2014). At 3-6 yrs of age, weight of the infant was similar in the control and preeclampsia groups and is shown in Table.5

The height, head and chest circumference were lower in preeclampsia group at day 3 ($p<0.01$) and 1.5 mo ($p<0.01$) of lactation as compared to control group. Further, at 2.5, 3.5, 6 mo of lactation and at 3-6 yrs of age, above growth measures were similar in control and preeclampsia groups (Table. 5).

Table 5: Anthropometric Measurement in Children at 3-6 yrs of Age

Growth Measures	Control (n=46)	Preeclampsia (n=39)
Weight (kg)	**14.66 ± 1.67**	**14.75 ± 2.42**
Length (cm)	**103.92 ± 4.50**	**101.95 ± 5.91**
HC (cm)	**47.53 ± 4.95**	**47.94 ± 1.29**
CC (cm)	**48.68 ± 1.96**	**48.47 ± 2.95**

HC: Head circumference; **CC**: Chest circumference. Values are expressed as Mean ± SD.

5.15.1 Standard Score of Index of the KABC-II

There were no statistical difference between the score of Atlantis, Word order, Conceptual thinking, Face recognition and Expressive vocabulary in both the groups (Table 6). The standard score of conceptual thinking was significantly lower ($p<0.01$ for both) in children born preterm in the preeclampsia group as compared to children born at term (Fig. 31).

Table 6: Standard Score of Index of the KABC-II at 3-6 yrs of Age

Name of Subtest	Control (n=46)	Preeclampsia (n=39)
Atlantis	9.43 ± 2.32	9.36 ± 2.68
Word order	9.17 ± 2.30	8.95 ± 1.77
Conceptual thinking	7.61 ± 2.45	6.97 ± 2.48
Face recognition	7.83 ± 2.60	7.64 ± 2.37
Expressive vocabulary	6.65 ± 2.21	6.62 ± 1.81

Values are expressed as Mean ± SD

Figure 31: Standard Score of Index of the KABC-II in Preeclampsia Groups based on Gestation

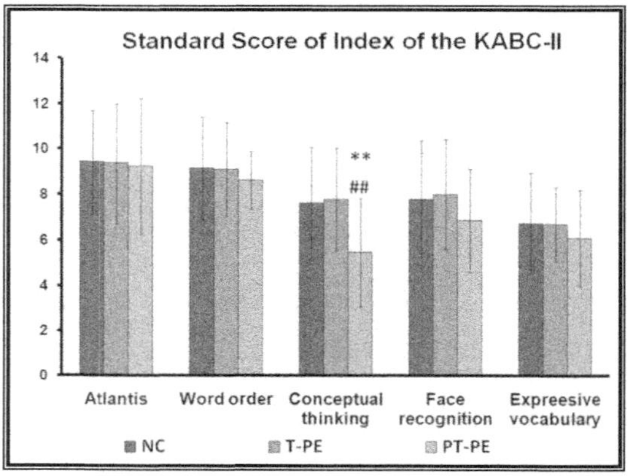

NC: Normotensive control; **PE:** Preeclampsia; **T-PE:** Term PE; **PT-PE**-Preterm PE

Values are Mean ± SD; p: significance. **$p<0.01$ when compared to normotensive control; ##$p<0.05$ when compared to T-PE

5.16 Associations of Milk Fatty Acids with Cognition of Children

There was a negative association between milk LA levels at birth and face recognition (r=-0.316, p=0.060, n=36) in the control group. However, no association was seen in the preeclampsia group.

At 6 mo, milk SFA levels were positively associated expressive vocabulary (r=0.399, p=0.053, n=24) in the control group. This was not seen in preeclampsia group. In contrast, at 6 mo, ALA (r=-0.756, p=0.000, n=17) and omega 3 fatty acids (r=-0.756, p=0.000, n=17) were negatively associated with expressive vocabulary only in preeclampsia group.

CHAPTER 6
DISCUSSION

This section discusses the findings on the levels of various components in breast milk in women with preeclampsia and compares them with normotensive control women. The possible implications on infant growth and cognition are also discussed.

6.1 Maternal Plasma and Milk Fatty Acid Levels in Control and preeclampsia Groups at Various Time Points of Lactation

This is the first report to examine plasma and breast milk fatty acid profiles in women with preeclampsia. The maternal plasma levels of ALA, DHA and total omega 3 fatty acids were lower in the preeclampsia group as compared to normotensive control group. The lower levels of these fatty acids may be either due to changes in the diet, metabolism or transport of fatty acids. Our earlier study from the department indicates that the frequency of consumption of omega-3 fatty acid rich foods is similar between the preeclampsia and normotensive control group (Kulkarni et al. 2011; Wadhwani et al. 2014). It is therefore likely that the reduction in maternal plasma DHA levels may be due to altered metabolism in women with preeclampsia.

Our data has shown a decrease in AA and DHA levels from day 3 to 6 mo of lactation and is consistent with a reported longitudinal study which has also demonstrated that the milk DHA and AA gradually decrease from colostrum to mature milk (Chen et al. 1997). Furthermore, the levels of both the precursors (LA and ALA) were lower and the products (AA and DHA) were higher in the milk in both the groups at day 3 (closer to colostrum) compared to milk at later time points (mature milk). Increased levels of milk AA at day 3 may improve the growth of the newborns. It is well known that AA is an important nutrient factor for growth in early postnatal life (Much et al. 2013). Reports indicate that milk AA levels may not be mediating inflammation because human milk contains high anti-inflammatory than pro-inflammatory lipid mediators (Takamoto et al. 1995).

LCPUFA such as AA and DHA are synthesized by elongation/desaturation of precursors like LA and ALA, respectively. Desaturases are the enzymes which regulate the unsaturated fatty acid biosynthesis and are mainly present in liver. It has been reported that fatty acid desaturase enzyme activity in newborns is low (Innis, 2007). Current data shows increased milk levels of both LCPUFA precursors (LA and ALA) and reduced products (AA and DHA) from day 3 to 6 mo of lactation. At later time points, the levels of AA and DHA decrease possibly because of reduced need for products (AA and DHA) due to increased conversion ability of the infant. It has been mentioned that the infants probably can synthesize additional LCPUFA from the LA and ALA contents of human milk (Heird, 2001).

The levels of DHA in breast milk remain higher in mothers with preeclampsia as compared to controls throughout lactation except at 2.5 mo. We have earlier reported higher milk DHA levels at postnatal day 3 in women with preeclampsia in spite of its lower plasma DHA levels in mother which is consistent with the data reported by us earlier in another cohort (Dangat et al. 2010). The levels of milk DHA in the current study are similar to the levels reported in countries like Nepal (Glew et al. 2001) and Bangladesh (Yakes et al. 2011). Milk DHA levels in our study is similar to Sudanese mothers whose diet is devoid of fish products (Nyuar et al. 2010) and American Indian women with low DHA intake (Glew et al. 2011). In contrast, milk DHA levels were slightly higher in Cuba (Krasevec et al. 2002). A study on milk samples from 9 different countries has revealed that milk SFA and MUFA composition is constant but PUFA like DHA is highly variable (Yuhas et al. 2006). A study from China reveals that mothers in coastal area of china showed higher DHA status of milk (Peng et al. 2009). Milk DHA showed a positive correlation with dietary DHA intake (Glew et al. 2011). This suggests maternal diet and fatty acid metabolism plays a critical role in determining the DHA status of the mother. The frequency of consumption of ALA, DHA and omega 3 rich foods was similar in both the normotensive control and preeclampsia groups throughout the period of lactation.

Increased milk DHA levels in current study level may be probably due to increased expression of sterol regulatory element binding proteins (SREBP-1) in the mammary glands which in turn increases the expression of delta-5 desaturase and delta-6 desaturase ultimately resulting in increased DHA synthesis. Our study subjects are predominantly vegetarian and have lower levels as compared to higher levels in countries with higher sea food diet. In our study, the mean milk DHA levels decreased from day 3 to 6 mo of lactation in both preeclampsia and control groups. Higher milk DHA levels in colostrum compared to mature milk have been reported in both term and preterm mothers (Berenhauser et al. 2012). This is also consistent with the reports from lactating Italian mothers (Agostoni, 2005). The levels of AA in the present study were in the ideal range which has been recently reported (Antonakou et al. 2013).

Our study suggests that the need of LCPUFA, especially DHA, can be satisfied in healthy normotensive mothers by breastfeeding during early lactating period. Reports suggest that long term and short term maternal diet and fatty acid status influences the milk fatty acid status (Del Prado et al. 2001; Innis, 2007). In current study, higher milk DHA levels in mothers with preeclampsia may be due to altered metabolism of fatty acids. In addition to maternal diet, breast milk fatty acid composition is also dependent on mobilization of endogenous stores of fatty acids and *de novo* synthesis of fatty acids by liver or breast tissue (Sabel et al. 2012).

Our data suggests that milk LCPUFA are altered in preeclampsia. Further, LCPUFA could plausibly influence the growth especially in children born to mothers with preeclampsia. Thus, animal studies should investigate the mechanisms involved in the mammary gland synthesis of LCPUFA and their role in growth and development of offspring in future.

6.2 Maternal Plasma and Milk Neurotrophin Levels in Control and preeclampsia Groups at Various Time Points of Lactation

Recent reports suggest that breastfeeding is associated with improved cognitive development (Quigley et al. 2012). These beneficial effects on neurodevelopment have mainly been attributed to the presence of LCPUFA especially DHA in human milk (Huppi, 2008; Valentine et al. 2013). We have demonstrated that the levels of brain neurotrophins in animals can be improved as a consequence of omega 3 fatty acid supplementation (Sable et al. 2012).

However, there are very limited reports available on the levels of neurotrophins in human milk. A recent study indicates that the growth factors that are present in all human milk samples at various concentrations may support the development of the nervous system (Fichter et al. 2011). Presence of NGF in milk has also been reported earlier in the mouse (Grueters et al. 1985), rat (Gorin et al. 1979) and humans (Wright and Gaull, 1983). A report suggests that BDNF can be added to the list of bioactive factors (e.g. IL- 206 1b, IL-2, IL-4, IL-5, lactoferrin, transferrin) present in human milk (Li et al. 2011). However, it still remains unclear whether milk neurotrophins can get altered in pregnancy complications like preeclampsia.

In the present study, the levels of BDNF are highest at 3 day in the preeclampsia group as compared to the control group. Our data also shows that the milk BDNF levels show a higher trend throughout lactation except at 1.5 mo in preeclampsia group as compared to controls. The significant quantitative differences in BDNF at several time points during lactation between controls and preeclampsia probably indicate that the milk programming by mother's breast is altered by preeclampsia. It is likely that these changes are most likely adaptive changes of mother and some of these changes are not normalized even up to 6 mo. There is a report which indicates no change in milk BDNF levels at days 3, 10, 30, and 90 after parturition (Li et al. 2011). The levels of BDNF in the present study are lower than that reported by Li et al. (2011) and may be attributed to the difference in methodology. In the present study, BDNF levels were analyzed from whole milk. There has been no evidence that BDNF in human milk are derived entirely from the serum or mammary gland cells (Li et al. 2011).

Our data indicating reduced maternal plasma BDNF levels in preeclampsia probably suggest a role for BDNF in placental development. There are no studies which have examined the levels of milk BDNF in preeclampsia. Studies in mice have demonstrated altered mRNA and protein expression of BDNF and its receptor TrkB in the mammary glands where they play a role in cancer pathogenesis (Cameron and Foster, 2009). It is well established that neurotrophins and their receptors are also widely expressed in non neuronal tissues (Shibayama and Koizumi, 1996; Tessarollo and Lino, 1998). The mRNA and protein levels of BDNF are known to be altered by oxidative stress (Noble et al. 2011; Al-Ayadhi, 2012; Alzoubi et al. 2013). It has been reported that hypoxic conditions may affect the neurotrophin levels in rat embryos (Kim et al. 2004).

We have earlier reported increased oxidative stress and reduced LCPUFA in preeclampsia (Mehendale et al. 2008). It may be possible that the reduced polyunsaturated fatty acids alter the membrane fluidity resulting in receptor dysfunction in the mammary gland leading to increased milk BDNF levels. The source of BDNF in milk is not clear and there is a need for further research to understand the role of leukocyte-derived BDNF production.

In the current study, plasma levels of NGF were lower in women with preeclampsia but levels of milk NGF at day 3 were comparable to control. These results support our earlier studies where we have demonstrated reduced maternal plasma NGF levels in preeclampsia in another cohort (Kilari et al. 2011). It is known that children with preeclampsia are at increased risk of neurodevelopmental disorders (Cannon et al. 2008; Kajantie and Räikkönen, 2010). Reduced neurogenesis and neurite loss is a feature of neurodevelopmental insults and neuronal injury.

In our study, NGF levels increase across lactation. Since NGF is known to play a crucial role in the process of angiogenesis (Karatzas et al. 2013), cell development as well as tissue proliferation (De Nicoló et al. 2013), increments in milk NGF may play a role in infant growth and development during lactation. In this study, milk NGF levels were lower in preeclampsia group as compared to control group throughout lactation. Composition of bioactive components like growth factors of breast milk are suggested to be lower based in mothers associated with oxidative stress (Gutikova, 2007). Our earlier study shows that preeclampsia is associated with increased oxidative stress (Mehendale et al. 2008) which may partly explain the lower levels of milk NGF in preeclampsia group.

Neurotrophins such as NGF and BDNF are known to control the neuronal apoptosis during brain development and play an important role in neuronal differentiation, survival and growth of neurons (Barichello et al. 2013) and also modulate synaptic plasticity in normal and pathological conditions (Siniscalco et al. 2011). Endogenous NGF is known to help in the regeneration of neuronal cells and promote sprouting (Jankowski et al. 2010; More et al. 2012). Reports indicate that higher serum BDNF levels in breast fed infants show a positive correlation with total behaviour rating scale which is indicative of improved cognition (Nassar et al. 2011). Although the exact function of neurotrophins in human milk is not yet certain, our findings suggest that the milk neurotrophins may be contributing to the postnatal neuronal growth and development of the babies born to mothers with preeclampsia. This is of significance since neurotrophins can cross the blood brain barrier and trigger neuronal downstream signaling effects in a highly localized region in the brain (Baseri et al. 2012). Animal studies have been initiated in the department to examine the effect of altered DHA levels on the expression of neurotrophins in the mammary gland.

Our data indicating higher breast milk BDNF and DHA levels in mothers with preeclampsia as compared to normotensive mothers suggests that breastfeeding infants born to mothers with preeclampsia would be beneficial. This study indicates that there is differential altered regulation of milk NGF and BDNF levels in women with preeclampsia. Our study with comprehensive analysis of both BDNF and NGF would be useful for determining optimal levels of neurotrophin contents of formulae for infants born to mothers with preeclampsia. Our data suggest that neurotrophins like BDNF could plausibly influence brain development and function especially in children born to mothers with preeclampsia. In the current study, while recruiting patients from the hospital, details about education, parity was recorded and was found to be similar. This study is important since this allows us to propose and test the hypothesis which reflects the pathophysiology and not the complications of confounds of other factors. Also, this cohort represents a large percent of the Indian population. We are now recruiting women from the higher socioeconomic class in an urban population. We believe that the findings obtained from this study will help us to better understand the interactions with environmental factors and eventually interaction with genetic factors. However, one limitation of the study is that these findings cannot be generalized to the higher socioeconomic group. Further studies should examine the protein and mRNA levels of neurotrophins in the mammary gland to understand the mechanisms involved in the regulation of the milk neurotrophins using animal models.

6.3 Associations of Milk Fatty Acids with Baby Characteristics during lactation

In our study, milk AA levels were negatively associated with baby weight at 1.5 and 3.5 mo and milk DHA levels were negatively associated with baby length at 3.5 mo during lactation in the preeclampsia group. In contrast, few studies have shown that total milk omega 3 PUFA in normal population was positively associated with infant weight gain (Tinoco et al. 2009), motor, mental and behavioral developments (Sabel et al. 2012). A review discusses the controversial reports on fatty acid supplementation effects on neurodevelopment in both animal and human studies (Davis-Bruno et al. 2011).

6.4 Levels of Milk Metabolites

The present study for the first time reports various metabolites in breast milk in mothers with preeclampsia and compares them with normotensive control women at day 3 and at the 6 month of lactation. The key finding of current study suggests that milk metabolites varied between control and preeclampsia groups. In addition, at 6 mo of lactation, few metabolites such as alpha and beta lactose, glutamate, glutamine, glycine, phosphocholine, and glycerophosphocholine levels increased as compared to day 3 of lactation in the control group. However, in the preeclampsia group, only glycerophosphocholine level increased at 6 mo of lactation. The levels of acetone, acetate and creatine decreased in both the groups at 6 mo as compared to day 3 of lactation. In the current study, the milk components were similar at day 3 in control and preeclampsia women. Reports suggest that the carbohydrate, fat, proteins and energy concentrations in breast milk are significantly higher in women delivering preterm as compared to mothers delivering at term (Armaforte et al. 2010; Bauer and Gerss, 2011;

Longini et al. 2014; Sundekilde et al. 2016). In this study, the gestation in the preeclampsia group was significantly lower as compared to the control group. Hence, the data for milk metabolites at day 3 was adjusted for gestation. However, the levels of milk metabolites did not change after adjusting for gestation. In the present study, the altered metabolic profiles were determined by two methods (i) multivariate analysis of spectral bins, and (ii) by comparing the concentration of the metabolites. However, the concentration of metabolites could be determined only for unique peaks which did not show any spectral overlap, thus it was limited by the number of metabolites which could be quantitated. The concentration of metabolites was determined to obtain a more accurate quantitative measure of the levels of metabolites that may help in ascertaining the alterations in the metabolic pathways associated with the disease. Alternatively, binning of the data would provide only relative levels of the metabolites, but it was possible to explore the entire spectral width using this method. Thus, multivariate data analysis applied on 200 spectral bins has provided information on those metabolites also for which it was not be possible to determine the concentration accurately. Since, binning of the data would provide only relative levels of the metabolites; we believe that the two types of analysis would provide complementary information.

Carbohydrates, especially lactose and oligosaccharides are the main components of human milk. Lactose, a major component of human milk acts as an osmotic agent and is synthesized in the Golgi body contributing to 7% of weight of the milk and is known to provide energy for the growth of infants (Neville, 1990). Lactose is also a source of galactose which is essential for the production of galactolipids which are essential for the central nervous system development (Akré, 1990). In the current study, the levels of lactose increased at 6 mo as compared to day 3 of lactation in the control group. However, this increase was not observed in the preeclampsia group and the levels were lower as compared to controls at 6 mo of lactation. Human milk contains >200 different HMO's and so far only >100 have been identified (Bode, 2012). However, the absolute concentration of these metabolite peaks from HMO cannot be determined due to overlap with other peaks. Loading plots obtained from multivariate data analysis showed that HMO's contributed for group separation on PLS-DA plots. In the univariate analysis milk HMO levels did not show significant difference between day 3 and 6 mo of lactation in both control as well as in preeclampsia groups. This might be due to large variation in the levels of HMO's within the group as it was evident from the high standard deviation seen for these metabolites.

Our data showed an increase in free amino acids such as glutamate, glutamine and glycine levels at 6 mo as compared to day 3 of lactation. In contrast, no increase was seen in the milk of mothers with preeclampsia indicating an insufficient supply of these amino acids to the infants. Earlier reports indicate that glutamate, glutamine and glycine levels increase with advancing lactation (Agostoni et al. 2000; Singh et al. 2004; Zhang et al. 2013). Glutamate is known to act as an important neurotransmitter that plays a key role in long-term potentiation, synaptic plasticity and is important for cognitive functions like learning and memory (Sapolsky, 2005; Hertz et al. 1999). Our findings are of significance since it is known that babies born to mothers with preeclampsia are associated with fetal growth restriction (Srinivas et al. 2009) and cognitive disorders in later life (Many et al. 2003).

Our data indicates that the levels of glycine remain unchanged in both the preeclampsia and control groups at day 3 of lactation but showed a decrease in the preeclampsia group at 6 mo of lactation. Reports indicated that plasma glycine levels do not differ in women with preeclampsia as compared to control (Kremenski et al. 1990). Glycine and glutamate are known to be critical for glutathione synthesis which is the most abundant intracellular antioxidant and is necessary for combating oxidative stress in humans. Evidence indicates that glutathione may be a possible marker to predict the risk of preeclampsia (Siddiqui et al. 2013). We have earlier reported increased oxidative stress in women with preeclampsia (Mehendale et al. 2008).

In this study, glycerophosphocholine levels in milk increased at 6 mo as compared to day 3 of lactation. However, glycerophosphocholine levels were lower in the preeclampsia group as compared to control at 6 mo of lactation. It has been demonstrated that choline gets rapidly metabolized to phosphocholine for the formation of glycerophosphocholine in the mammary gland (Kennedy et al. 1956). Further, phosphocholine levels increased from day 3 to 6 mo only in the control group but not in the preeclampsia group. There are no studies reporting the levels of milk phosphocholine and glycerophosphocholine in preeclampsia. Glycerophosphocholine and phosphocholine are formed during phosphatidylcholine metabolism by the action of phospholipases A2 (PLA2). PLA2 is a circulating enzyme which plays a central role in inflammatory responses and also in oxidative stress (Cavigiolio and Jayaraman, 2014). The lower levels of milk glycerophosphocholine in preeclampsia as compared to the control group at 6 mo may be due to a disturbed PLA2 activity in the mammary gland in mothers with preeclampsia.

Milk also contains metabolites which are associated with tricarboxylic acid cycle intermediates, glycolysis, and products of energy metabolism (citrate, acetone, creatine, and phosphocreatine) (Smilowitz et al. 2013). Our data demonstrates a decrease in citrate levels in the preeclampsia group as lactation progress. This indicates that there may be an impaired energy metabolism in babies born to mothers with preeclampsia.

Studies indicate that maternal diet can influence the composition of human milk (Karmarkar and Ramakrishnan, 1959; Nommsen et al. 1991; Rakicioğlu et al. 2006). Milk fatty acid composition has been shown to vary between vegetarian and non-vegetarian mothers (Jiang et al. 2016). In contrast, a recent study reports no association between maternal dietary constituents and the breast milk components during lactation (Jiang et al. 2016). The current study demonstrates that vegetarian or non-vegetarian diets did not influence milk metabolite levels. However, studies need to confirm these findings on larger numbers.

6.5 Anthropometric Measurements in Children from Birth to 3-6 yrs of age

It has been suggested that the presence of maternal hypertension during pregnancy may affect breastfeeding and thereby early infant growth (Baulon et al.

2005). In the present study, birth weight, length, head and chest circumference was lower at day 3 and 1.5 mo of lactation in infants born to mothers with preeclampsia. A common consequence of preeclampsia is reduced nutritional supply to the fetus due to altered placental development that may compromise the flow of nutrients and oxygen to the fetus, and similarly reduces transportation of waste from the fetus (Ogland et al. 2009).

There was no significant change in these growth measures at 3-6 mo of age. A retrospective cohort study from China demonstrated that IUGR babies born to mothers with pregnancy induced hypertension had lower infant weight and significant 'catch-up' growth at 28 and 42 days postpartum (Baulon et al. 2005). Several studies have shown an inverse association between birth weight and BMI later in life, and it has been suggested that low birth weight is an indicator of intrauterine factors that may alter the developing fetus to a phenotype that will tend to conserve energy (Rogers, 2003; Gluckman and Hanson, 2006,).

In our study, at the age of 3 to 6 yrs, all the growth measures of the children were comparable between control and preeclampsia groups. Preeclampsia has been associated with low birth weight and later associated with the catch-up growth in infancy and early childhood (Ogland et al. 2009, Byberg et al. 2017). Studies on very premature children born small for gestational age have reported that they have catch-up in linear growth (after 6 yrs of age) (Druet and Ong, 2008). In contrast, Tenhola et al. report that offspring of preeclamptic and normotensive pregnancies did not differ by body size (BMI, weight or sub-scapular skin folds) at 12 yrs of age (Tenhola et al. 2003).

6.6 Cognitive Performance of Children

In our study, the outcomes of 5 developmental tests such as Atlantis, Word order, Conceptual thinking, Face recognition and Expressive vocabulary assessed by Kaufman Assessment Battery for Children (KABC II) were not different in children born to mothers with preeclampsia and normotensive control women. The higher levels of DHA and BDNF observed in the breast milk of mothers may have a beneficial effect. In accordance with our study, it has been reported that at

18 mo of age, cognitive function, assessed by the Bayley Scales, was not associated with maternal preeclampsia. The authors concluded that hypertension during gestation could even be protective (Silveira et al. 2007). A retrospective cohort study showed that maternal hypertensive disorders are not associated with adverse neurodevelopmental outcomes at 2–3 yrs of age (Matic et al. 2017).

In our study, possibly the age of 3-6 yrs is too young to find behavioral problems, therefore larger studies with longer follow-up are needed to further define this relationship. A reduced cognitive performance in adult men (Ehrenstein et al. 2009) and in 20 yr old male offspring (Tuovinen et al. 2012) exposed to gestational hypertensive disorders has been reported earlier. These findings indicate that neurodevelopmental studies addressing the influence of preeclampsia on cognitive function at 3-6 yrs are warranted.

Preeclampsia is associated with adverse pregnancy outcomes, including intrauterine growth restriction and preterm birth, all of which are associated with increased neurodevelopment delays. So, in our study women with preeclampsia were further categorized into women delivering at term (≥37 weeks gestation) (term preeclampsia) and women delivering preterm (<37 weeks gestation) (preterm preeclampsia) groups. Our findings indicate that the score of conceptual thinking was significantly lower in children born preterm to women with preeclampsia. The subtest conceptual thinking measures classification ability in nonverbal format. These findings indicate lower classification ability of children born to women with preeclampsia delivering preterm. Our findings suggest that gestational age contributes to the neurodevelopmental outcomes in children.

SUMMARY

The present thesis entitled "Breast milk components and neurodevelopmental risk in children born to mothers with preeclampsia" examined the levels of fatty acids, neurotrophins and various other metabolites in the breast milk of women with preeclampsia and normotensive control women. Further, this study also reports the growth and cognitive performance in children at 3-6 year of age.

Breast milk is the primary source of nutrition to the newborn. It contains wide range of nutrients and other bioactive components which play a vital role in the growth and development of infant. Pregnancy complications such as pregnancy induced hypertension; preeclampsia and gestational diabetes mellitus are known to affect lactogenesis. An earlier cross-sectional study in our department has demonstrated altered maternal and placental angiogenesis in women with preeclampsia. This may also influence mammary gland development and thereby lactogenesis. Children born to mothers with preeclampsia are at increased risk for behavioural problems during childhood. Several studies have shown the association of breastfeeding with better neurodevelopment outcome. It is likely that the constituents of human milk play a vital role in early brain development.

Long chain polyunsaturated fatty acids (LCPUFA) are essential for normal brain development and are also involved in many neurobiological processes. In neurotrophins specifically, brain derived neurotrophic factor (BDNF) is involved in different aspects of learning and memory processing and nerve growth factor (NGF) is critical for enhancing memory formation and facilitating hippocampal long-term potentiation.

Recent reports indicate that milk components change over the course of lactation due to time dependent programmed requirement for the child development. We have earlier reported higher breast milk DHA levels in women with preeclampsia on day 3 of lactation. DHA is known to regulate the expression of neurotrophins and together they play a vital role in neurodevelopment and cognitive performance. However, the levels of these nutrients and growth factors across various stages of lactation are not studied so far. The present study for the first time reports the levels of breast milk components (fatty acids, neurotrophins and various other metabolites) at various time points of lactation in women with preeclampsia. The association of these milk components with growth and cognitive performance of children is also reported.

Hypothesis

"Milk components will be altered in preeclampsia which will affect cognitive performance in children"

Study Design

This study was conducted at Interactive Research School for Health Affairs (IRSHA) and patients were recruited from Departments of Obstetrics & Gynecology, Bharati Hospital and Research Center, Pune. The study was approved by the Bharati Vidyapeeth Medical College Institutional Ethics Committee. Singleton pregnant women with preeclampsia (n=101) and normotensive control women (n=144) were recruited at the time of delivery. Mothers and their babies were followed-up at day 3, and 1.5 mo, 2.5 mo, 3.5 mo and 6 mo post delivery. The anthropometry (weight and length, head and chest circumference) of the infant was recorded at all time points during lactation. Maternal plasma samples were collected at delivery. Milk samples were collected at various time points during lactation i.e at day 3 and 1.5, 2.5, 3.5 and 6 mo post delivery. Fatty acids, neurotrophins and other metabolites were analyzed from maternal plasma (at delivery) and from breast milk (at different time points of lactation). Anthropometric measurements were recorded by standard techniques and cognitive performance was examined using the Kaufman assessment battery (KABC II) in children at 3-6 yrs of age.

Key Findings of the Study

The present study suggests that there is a differential regulation of fatty acids and neurotrophins in the breast milk of women with preeclampsia and are associated with growth parameters of children. It also highlights a role of NGF and BDNF in human milk for postnatal brain development of infants. In spite of altered milk components in women with preeclampsia, there was no change in the cognitive performance of the children born to mothers with preeclampsia compared to children born to normotensive control mothers.

The study demonstrates the following interesting findings:

Breast Milk Fatty acids Levels across Lactation

1. The breast milk levels of docosahexaenoic acid (DHA) were significantly higher at day 3, 1.5 and 3.5 mo of lactation (in spite of lower maternal plasma DHA) in women with preeclampsia as compared to normotensive control women. It is likely that there could be an adaptive mechanism to synthesize LCPUFA through increased expression of sterol regulatory element binding proteins (SREBP) in the mammary glands.

2. There was an increase in the milk levels of both the LCPUFA precursors (LA and ALA) and decrease in the levels of products (AA and DHA) from day 3 to 6 mo of lactation in both the control and preeclampsia groups. This may possibly because of reduced need for products due to increased conversion ability of the infant to synthesize LCPUFA.

3. The levels of milk DHA and total omega 3 fatty acids at day 3 of lactation were higher in normotensive control women consuming a non-vegetarian diet as compared to women consuming a vegetarian diet. However, such changes were not observed in the preeclampsia group.

Breast Milk Neurotrophins Levels across Lactation

1. Milk NGF levels were similar while milk BDNF levels were higher at day 3 of lactation in the preeclampsia as compared to control group. Our results indicate a differential regulation of milk NGF and BDNF levels in women with preeclampsia.

2. The levels of both NGF and BDNF in control and preeclampsia groups showed very different longitudinal patterns. There was an increase in the

levels of milk NGF from day 3 to 6 mo of lactation while no such pattern was observed for BDNF levels.

Metabolites in the Breast milk

1. The levels of milk metabolites were similar at day 3 of lactation in both the control and preeclampsia groups.

2. The levels of alpha and beta-lactose, glycine, glycerophosphocholine, glutamate, glutamine and phosphocholine increased at the 6 month as compared to day 3 of lactation in the control group. However, such change was not observed in preeclampsia group.

3. The levels of acetate, acetone, creatine decreased at 6 month as compared to day 3 of lactation in both the groups. The levels of oligosaccharides were similar between groups and also similar at day 3 and at the 6 month of lactation in both the groups.

Anthropometry and Cognitive performance of the Children

1. The birth weight, length, head and chest circumference was lower in infants born to mothers with preeclampsia suggesting intrauterine growth retardation which is a major consequence of preeclampsia.

2. The anthropometric measurements were similar in the children at 3-6 yrs of age between control and preeclampsia groups.

3. The cognitive abilities of children assessed by analyzing the standard scores of subtests such as atlantis, word order, conceptual thinking, face recognition and expressive vocabulary were not different among the children born to women with preeclampsia and normotensive control women.

4. The standard score of conceptual thinking was significantly lower in children born to preeclampsia women delivering preterm as compared to normotensive control and women with preeclampsia delivering at term.

Associations of Milk Fatty Acids and Neurotrophins with Growth and Cognition in Children

1. There was a positive association between milk AA and baby length in the control group.

2. Milk SFA levels were positively associated expressive vocabulary in the control group. However, such associations were not observed in the preeclampsia group.

Implications

Lactation is beneficial to the health of mothers and their infants. Globally the rate of exclusive breastfeeding continues to be sub-optimal and the data is scarce on women affected by preeclampsia. Preeclampsia is a complication affecting 8-10% of all pregnancies. Babies born to mothers with preeclampsia are at higher risk for metabolic and cognitive disorders. There is a potential relationship between preeclampsia and delayed onset of lactogenesis. Our data suggests that milk LCPUFA and neurotrophins are altered in women with preeclampsia. Neurotrophins and LCPUFA are critical for brain growth and development of the offspring. The present study with comprehensive analysis of all essential fatty acids present in the plasma and breast milk of mothers with preeclampsia would be useful for determining the optimal LCPUFA content required for growth of infant.

Limitations

The limitation of the study is the small number of mothers and children participating in follow up sessions at different stages of lactation. Breast milk volume was not recorded in the present study. This study, examined the role of breast milk components in lower socioeconomic group. There is a need to examine the breast milk components in the higher socioeconomic group.

Societal Relevance

The current study provides some evidence on the beneficial roles of breast milk LCPUFA and neurotrophins on cognitive performance in children. Our findings support the existing policies to promote breastfeeding for 6 mo to improve infant growth. This study also provides important clues which would help to optimize the levels of these vital constituents in mother's milk or proper supplementation to improve cognitive performance in children.

Future Prospects

Animal studies should investigate the mechanisms involved in the mammary gland synthesis of BDNF, NGF and LCPUFA and their role in the growth and development of offspring. Further, there is a need to carry out long-term follow-up studies in children to examine their risk for neurodevelopmental outcome and cardio-metabolic risk.

CONCLUSION

This study for the first time reports the levels of long chain polyunsaturated fatty acids (LCPUFA), neurotrophins and other metabolites in breast milk in women with preeclampsia across lactation and their association with growth and cognitive performance in the children.

The present study for the first time demonstrates several novel and interesting findings:

1. The levels of DHA were higher in the breast milk in mothers with preeclampsia as compared to control group throughout lactation in spite of lower maternal plasma DHA.

2. Maternal milk BDNF levels were higher while NGF levels were lower in mothers with preeclampsia as compared to control group suggesting differential regulation of neurotrophins in preeclampsia.

3. Milk metabolites varied between control and preeclampsia groups.

4. The anthropometric measures at birth (weight, length, head and chest circumference) were lower in babies born to mothers with preeclampsia. However,there was no change in these growth measures at 3-6 yrs of age.

5. The outcomes of five developmental subtests such as atlantis, word order, conceptual thinking, face recognition and expressive vocabulary were similar in both the groups. However, conceptual thinking was lower in children born preterm in women with preeclampsia.

6. The present study highlights the need to breastfeed all babies especially those born to mothers with preeclampsia for optimal growth and cognitive performance.

9 781805 251989

Printed by BoD™in Norderstedt, Germany